THE TALE OF HEALER
MIGUEL PERDOMO NEIRA

THE TALE OF HEALER
MIGUEL PERDOMO NEIRA

Medicine, Ideologies, and
Power in the Nineteenth-Century Andes

DAVID SOWELL

A Scholarly Resources Inc. Imprint
Wilmington, Delaware

Scholarly Resources Inc.
104 Greenhill Avenue
Wilmington, DE 19805-1897
www.scholarly.com

Library of Congress Cataloging-in-Publication Data

Sowell, David, 1952–
    The tale of healer Miguel Perdomo Neira : medicine, ideologies,
and power in the nineteenth-century Andes / David Sowell.
        p. ; cm. — (Latin American silhouettes series)
    Includes bibliographical references and index.
    ISBN 0-8420-2826-9 (cloth : alk. paper) — ISBN 0-8420-
2827-7 (pbk. : alk. paper)
    1. Perdomo Neira, Miguel. 2. Traditional medicine—Andes
Region—History—19th century. 3. Indians of South America—
Medicine—Andes Region—History—19th century. 4. Social
medicine—Andes Region—History—19th century. I. Title.
II. Latin American silhouettes.
    [DNLM: 1. Perdomo Neira, Miguel. 2. Medicine, Traditional—
history—Colombia. 3. Medicine, Traditional—history—Ecuador.
4. History of Medicine, 19th Cent.—Colombia. 5. History of
Medicine, 19th Cent.—Ecuador. 6. Knowledge, Attitudes, Practice—Colombia. 7. Knowledge, Attitudes, Practice—Ecuador.
8. Politics—Colombia. 9. Politics—Ecuador. WZ 309 S73lt 2001]
    RA645.37.A5 S69 2001
    610'.98'09034—dc21   00-067984

In memory of Debbie,
whose presence is sorely missed

ACKNOWLEDGMENTS

This project has been supported by friends, family, and institutions. I gratefully acknowledge the financial backing of the William J. and Frances Nyce Fund of Juniata College that sustained part of the research for this project. Initial research was conducted while I was supported by a Fulbright Fellowship. Many of the ideas developed in this book were stimulated by a National Endowment for the Humanities Institute on "The Contributions of the History of Medicine to Social History," hosted by the Center for the Study of Society and Medicine of the College of Physicians and Surgeons of Columbia University. The participants at this seminar demonstrated the value of an interdisciplinary perspective on the social history of medicine. The staffs at the Archivo Central del Cauca (Popayán), the Biblioteca Nacional de Colombia (Bogotá), the Biblioteca Luis Angel Arango (Bogotá), the Biblioteca Municipal de Quito, the Archivo Municipal de Historia (Quito), the Fundación Biblioteca Ecuatoriana Aurelio Espinosa Polit (Quito), and the Biblioteca Municipal de Guayaquil proved extremely helpful in tracking down the dispersed evidence that sustains this volume. Victor Uribe-Uran assisted in collecting documents in Antioquia. Conversations with Diana Obregón Torres, Emilio Quevedo V., Michael Henderson, and Don Stevens provided important insights for me, and evaluators at Scholarly Resources offered challenging comments that have improved the book.

My family has lived with this project through its fitful life and has helped in many ways, despite the fact that my research and writing have taken time away from more enjoyable activities. Both Chris and Emily have been helpful in the editing of the text, though I took fewer of their suggestions than I probably should have. Their comments, along with those of colleagues, have been most appreciated. The errors and shortcomings that remain are my own responsibility.

ABOUT THE AUTHOR

David Sowell is associate professor of history at Juniata College, Huntingdon, Pennsylvania, where he has taught since 1989. He earned his doctorate in Latin American history from the University of Florida in 1986 under the direction of David Bushnell. Professor Sowell's research on the social history of the northern Andean region is presented in *The Early Colombian Labor Movement: Artisans and Politics in Bogotá, 1832–1919* (1993), as well as in various articles and book chapters. His work has largely focused on the nineteenth century, with an emphasis on artisans, political culture, social violence, and the social history of medicine.

CONTENTS

INTRODUCTION

Writing a book is a long, laborious process that often takes unex-
pected twists and turns as new documents or research findings
lead the author down unanticipated paths. This project was no exception. It began quite by accident almost twenty years ago while I was in
the midst of another research effort. In reading newspaper descriptions of 1872 Bogotá, I learned of a series of public confrontations
that centered upon Miguel Perdomo Neira, a traveling healer who
had recently arrived in the Colombian capital. Lay healers were seldom mentioned in the nineteenth-century press, which tended to
focus on partisan politics and other important issues of the day. Thus,
the appearance of a healer on the front pages of the national press
piqued my interest.

Riots occurred with a certain regularity throughout the nineteenth
century, often precipitated by political or socioeconomic crises. The
1872 riot involving Perdomo pitted professional physicians, medical
students, and certain members of the official political community
against broad segments of the city's populace. The immediate cause
for this social confrontation was an allegation made by a group of
physicians at the Hospital de Caridad (Hospital of Charity), charging
that Perdomo's medical incompetence had led to the death of one of
his patients. The healer's supporters feared that this charge, which
they thought to be false, would lead to his arrest and imprisonment.
Ardent Perdomistas marched through the Colombian capital, shouting threats against the professional medical community. They stoned
the houses of several doctors and forced at least one physician to flee
the city. After several hours of unrest, police and national guardsmen

restored order, aided by Perdomo's pleas that his supporters return to their homes. Shortly thereafter, the healer, now facing legal charges, left Bogotá.

Riots can provide important insights into social history, and analyses of these conflicts may illuminate tensions that are invisible in more tranquil periods. Officials almost always document a public disturbance, keeping records on who was arrested or killed and conducting judicial procedures to investigate the causes (and determine how to avoid future disturbances). People whose activities and opinions are generally absent from official records are often mentioned in documents related to such an event, offering the scholar opportunities for a more complete social analysis than is usually possible. For these reasons the 1872 riot caught my attention, leading me to seek out more information on Perdomo.

Nineteenth-century Colombian history was characterized by frequent conflicts between Conservatives and Liberals, members of the two major parties that still dominate the country's political landscape. My initial goal, therefore, was to determine the partisan dimensions of the riot, a research strategy that, though it revealed a clear partisan debate regarding Perdomo, provided little additional insight into the causes of the confrontation. An economic approach also shed very little light upon the nature of the disturbance, and focusing on the social groups active in the events of May 1872 proved helpful but, in the end, inconclusive.

Further readings of the press revealed that news of Perdomo's impending arrival had circulated in Conservative newspapers several weeks before he reached Bogotá. One account noted that his earlier visit to the town of Serrezuela had created an enormous public spectacle: "a multitude of curious and ill people were seen on all the roads that lead to the town. . . . The center of the plaza, the surrounding streets, and the patio and rooms of the house occupied by Perdomo were all filled with people."[1]

Several testimonials from those who had been cured by Perdomo were published in the same papers. Some came from places that he had visited early in the year, including one from Guaduas authored by the "poor and indigent" of the town. That note praised Perdomo's "Christian charity" for his refusal to accept payment for his medical treatments.[2] Another testimonial came from Serrezuela: "The undersigned residents of the district of Serrezuela . . . have the honor of directing to you this statement seeking your friendship, as a proof of our eternal gratitude. Nothing can compensate you for your care and attention . . . as a surgeon and doctor. . . . [Please know] that in Serrezuela you have admirers of your virtues; and that in whatever situation, in whatever circumstance, we will receive you with open arms, and that we will bless the day when you return to the land where you are so loved and venerated."[3]

Such testimonials demonstrated that Perdomo was an unusual individual who evoked widespread (and enthusiastic) public support because of his healing abilities. That he did not charge for his services, as noted in many reports, was an additional dimension of his public persona. His popularity and medical practices obviously played roles in the riot, but the broader implications of these factors became clear only over time.

Not all reports in the papers were favorable. The author of a letter from Guaduas, for instance, noted that many people were opposed to Perdomo and were "perplexed" by his cures.[4] Others cautioned Bogotanos to reserve their opinions of the healer until he arrived in the capital, suggesting that many medical professionals were skeptical of Perdomo's reputed abilities. Doctors at the hospital associated with the medical school of the Universidad Nacional reportedly wished to determine the "truth of what might be the secrets or prodigious abilities of Mr. Perdomo Neira"[5] by inviting him to the hospital, where they might observe him practice. As tensions in the city increased, the most prominent Liberal newspaper issued a lengthy editorial on the traveling healer, charging that he lacked scientific medical knowledge and that his medicine had harmed as many people as it had helped. The editorial claimed that the unrest in the city had been caused by blind, fanatical loyalty reminiscent of that seen in zealous adherents of the Catholic Church and that confrontations were little more than "a fight between *good sense and blind ignorance*."[6] Perdomo's printed response to the unrest in Bogotá included a brief overview of his history as a traveling healer and a retelling of a similar encounter in Quito, Ecuador, some five years earlier. There, too, professional physicians had expressed their antagonism toward him, charging that he was practicing medicine without a license. Police in Quito had arrested Perdomo, but he was freed amid concerns that similar social unrest would erupt.

As my research progressed, it became clear to me that medicine and healing were somehow central to the Bogotá riot, with supporters of the healer lined up against the leading physicians of the city. Standard medical histories of the era, however, were of limited value in illuminating possible reasons for the differences between the two factions. The historians of medicine focused their writings on the professional doctors who had criticized Perdomo, on the establishment of the school of medicine, and on innovations that had been introduced to the country from England or France. Most histories of Colombian medicine, in fact, said very little about the colonial period until the late 1700s, when "scientific" medicine was brought from Europe and when certain "enlightened" doctors began to practice in the major cities. With the accounts of the nineteenth century concentrated on prominent professional doctors, innovators, and the development of institutions,[7] few lay healers such as Perdomo were ever mentioned in these texts, even though they were the most numerous healers of the period.

The editorial comment about the struggle between "good sense and blind ignorance," it seemed to me, indicated that the conflicting attitudes toward Perdomo's abilities might prove to be a fruitful avenue of research. I knew that insofar as they originate in distinct medical systems,[8] contending healing ideologies often reveal fundamental social tensions.[9] And because illness often serves "as the source of a society's reflections about the ultimate nature of reality and about what matters most in life,"[10] illness and healing ideologies also reveal many of the truths that sustain social life. Readings on the social history of medicine suggested to me that the charismatic Perdomo's visit to Bogotá had exposed at least two different sets of medical belief. Thus, the 1872 riot, far from being a social disturbance with little meaning, became a window through which to view the contentions surrounding the major forces that reordered the society of nineteenth-century Latin America. In Colombia, the different medical systems were related to the bitter partisan struggle over the definition of the nation's moral and social fabric and were part of the "Great Transformation" of nineteenth-century Latin America.

Medical systems and medical knowledge do not exist in a vacuum, nor do they arise overnight. The colonization of the Americas by Spain produced a system that blended Catholic healing beliefs with indigenous and African medical ideologies, forming what I will refer to as a "colonial medical spectrum" in which Hispanic medicine dominated. Perdomo operated with this medical system. The professional doctors who criticized him, by contrast, believed in a rationalist, scientific medicine that some have labeled "biomedicine" because it places the supposedly neutral beliefs in biological laws at its core. Rationalist understandings had been developing in Western Europe since the sixteenth century, especially so during the 1700s and 1800s. Although rationalist medicine was introduced in the northern Andes in the late eighteenth century, its advocates did not acquire significant power until the mid-1800s. As that brand of medicine became scientific, it acquired an aura of modern truth that eclipsed other medical beliefs, which were generally described as "backward," "primitive," or "traditional." At their social and ideological cores, Hispanic medicine and rational medicine were fundamentally incompatible. Their respective supporters differed as to which ideology sustained a true interpretation of the world, and their disputes were made visible in the Bogotá riot and the conflicting interpretations of Perdomo.

The confrontation between distinct medical ideologies in 1872 Bogotá took place as scientific medicine was being institutionalized and authorized by the Colombian government. Today, though biomedicine dominates in the country, other medical systems are present as well, producing a social pattern referred to as "medical pluralism"— a situation in which several different medical systems operate within one society. Many regions of Latin America now exhibit medical pluralism. In some areas one medical ideology is so dominant that it defines the discourse, knowledge, and practices of medicine for an entire society. This ideological construction is not so complete in other areas, such as Ecuador or Colombia, where medical pluralism exists. Under medical pluralism, scientific medicine is sanctioned by the state as the "official medicine," even as other medical systems are routinely used by a large percentage of the population. Numerous studies describe how medical pluralism functions within contemporary Latin American societies, but little is known about its historical construction.[11]

The social and ideological conflicts that surrounded Perdomo in Bogotá and other towns reveal the potency of competitive medical ideologies. After generations in which Hispanic medicine had dominated the colonial medical spectrum, the rapid introduction and empowerment of scientific medicine sparked significant ideological and social battles in Latin America because, as in other areas with multiple medical systems, "the relationships between medical systems reveal an asymmetrical distribution of power in society; between a dominant medical system (with a marked tendency towards institutionalization and bureaucratization) and one or more subordinated medical systems."[12] Scientific medicine became official, and Hispanic medicine was sublimated into "popular" medicine. The power relations among medical systems are reflected in differentiated technologies, healers, ideologies, and sources of knowledge—all of which also illuminate the transformation of the traditional Hispanic intellectual, economic, and social norms that shaped contemporary Latin America.

According to the words of both the supporters and the critics of Perdomo, the Catholic Church stood at the center of the contention surrounding the traveling healer. Religion and healing are often joined socially; this was especially the case with the Church, which devoted much of its cult of sainthood to healing devotions. Catholic healing beliefs were deeply infused in the ideology of Hispanic medicine as practiced in the Americas. As we shall see, Perdomo acknowledged the moral and institutional potency of the Church in his writings, and he infused his healing with Catholic devotions. His own hacienda, San Juan de Dios, was named after the Order of Hospitallers, whose work he emulated.

This book represents a step toward the location of contentious medical ideologies within the Great Transformation of nineteenth-century Latin America that has linked the present to its colonial past. As critics of the colonial system gained social and political power, rationalism and liberalism became their predominant critical platforms. In the process, traditional society and especially the Church came under unceasing attack. Liberals reasoned that the social and political influence of the Church accounted for most of the "backwardness" that had to be curbed (if not eliminated) if Latin America were to progress. Economic policies of the 1840s and 1850s, influenced by liberalism, dramatically affected linkages with the capitalist system of the Atlantic community, bringing changes with both immediate and long-term social and economic consequences for the Latin American populace. After the mid-1800s the ruralization of political and economic power that took place during the Independence period was reversed as cities increased in size and importance. These cities regained their status as the nexus of social, economic, and cultural power, a position they had enjoyed during most of the colonial period. New ideological orientations, such as the belief in scientific medicine, were more apparent in the cities, which also displayed vanguard cultural trends. By the end of the twentieth century most of Latin America had adjusted to the profound transformative nature of these tendencies. But nineteenth-century Latin America witnessed severe contention as accustomed economic, social, political, and cultural norms came under attack from alien influences.

The greatest research challenge that I have confronted in this project has been the difficulty of finding information on Miguel Perdomo Neira. Nineteenth-century documents record relatively little on "the masses," especially in any kind of systematic fashion. Although Perdomo gained a certain amount of public prestige (and notoriety) that made him visible in the documents, many large information gaps exist. Several sources proved very valuable, however. Several dozen testimonials were printed either in newspapers or as pamphlets written by people defending his curing methods, shedding light on what his followers perceived to be his virtues. His critics also produced materials that provided an effective parallel to the supportive testimonials. In addition, a limited amount of information was available in judicial, notarial, and municipal archives. And finally, Perdomo's thoughts were recorded in a book that he published in 1872, *La iglesia católica en presencia del siglo XIX*. There, he provided a highly supportive overview of the role of the Church in society, as well as a short section on his healing ideology and a large collection of testimonials. The book offers considerable insight into his value system. It does not, however, make up for the fundamentally limited amount of documentary evidence on Perdomo himself.

The organization of this project has been particularly challenging. Ideally, Perdomo would command center stage, but the relative dearth of information on his life precluded that approach. Experiments with several organizational schemata led to this final iteration. Chapter 1 introduces some of the concepts used in the analysis but focuses on the characteristics of medical practices within the Hispanic colonial world. It offers an analytical overview of the Hispanic medical system in which Perdomo, most healers, and most residents operated in the early nineteenth century. Chapter 2 addresses scientific medicine and explores the manner by which it was introduced, gained power, and became institutionalized in Colombia and Ecuador. Chapter 3 describes the life and times of Perdomo, covering a period in which the conflicts between scientific and Hispanic medicine were made clear. Finally, Chapter 4 discusses the ideological contentions visible in Perdomo's life, the social power of healing, and the emergence of medical pluralism. I have purposely excluded from the analysis the correlation of political economy, social structures, and politics to the history of medicine. These and other variables could be incorporated in the present investigation without doing it harm and perhaps with great utility. But addressing these issues would have produced a fundamentally different work, one that awaits the further development of the history of medicine in nineteenth-century Latin America.

Readers will notice the relative preponderance of Colombian material as compared to that of Ecuador. There are several reasons for this bias. First, the nineteenth-century Colombian press and pamphlet tradition is wonderfully preserved at the Biblioteca Nacional de Colombia and at the Biblioteca Luis Angel Arango. Although their Ecuadorean counterparts have done a commendable job in collecting documents, there are simply fewer works to preserve. For most of the period under study, I suspect that six to eight times as much material was published in Bogotá than in Quito. Second, the 1872 incident in Bogotá was of a more profound nature than Perdomo's arrest in Quito five years earlier, and scientific medicine was far more firmly entrenched in Bogotá than in Quito, thus making the confrontation all the more remarkable. Third, the history of nineteenth-century medicine and science is developed to a much greater degree in regard to Colombia; medical anthropology, by contrast, has produced a wealth of information about contemporary Ecuador. And finally, my training as a Colombianist has undoubtedly made me more aware of Colombian sources.

1

HEALERS AND MEDICAL SYSTEMS IN ANDEAN AMERICA

Suffering humanity surrounds him,
and with untiring zeal throughout the day,
Perdomo practices high surgery
because he desires to relieve humanity's pain.

Is there no one in the town who does not believe,
and who upon seeing his deeds would not believe,
that his secrets have more value
than the expensive and deceitful pharmacopoeia?

His constant and delirious desire
is to calm the cruel illnesses of the poor:
Christian charity is his devotion;

And with his own natural gifts,
he fulfills the mission that Heaven gave him,
of giving life and health to mortals.

—Cardenio[1]

These lines describe Miguel Perdomo Neira, an empiric who practiced the healing arts throughout the northern Andes in the 1860s and 1870s. Empirics, sometimes called *curanderos* (healers), bleeders, or barbers, were lay healers who provided most of the health care to people at that time. Perdomo gained widespread popular acclaim throughout his travels because the drugs that he used purportedly enabled him to perform minor surgery without causing pain, swelling, or excessive bleeding. His supporters wrote numerous testimonials that expressed their gratitude for his ability to cure illnesses that had plagued them for years. They commented that Perdomo had lowered fevers that could not be reduced by other means, had alleviated breathing, vision, or urinary problems, and had removed cysts or tumors that had long troubled them. All reported that they had been cured at his hands—a majority by surgery, some by oral doses, and others by plasters. Many people said that they had seen other physicians before but without finding relief. A significant number testified that Perdomo had not charged for his services, in contrast to the doctors who had failed to cure them. Quite a few statements indicated that he was a godsend and that he acted in the spirit of Christian charity. (Many of these testimonials are reproduced in the Appendix.)

These testimonials offer valuable insights into the social history of medicine in a critical period of transition in Latin America. An examination of some of them helps to introduce an analytical framework that is useful for interpreting the healing ideologies of the mid-nineteenth century. A typical testimonial, published in May 1872 during Perdomo's visit to Bogotá, related that José María Devia "has suffered a grave infirmity in his right eye since his birth that has caused him extreme and immense pain; and that for all of these forty years, no one has been able to restore his health, in spite of visits to various doctors, until he presented himself to Dr. Miguel Perdomo Neira, who in the first moment that he saw him, offered to cure him; that [Perdomo] fulfilled this, and on this date he finds himself healthy and well, thanks to the grace of Providence."[2]

Devia's unspecified infirmity might be referred to as a "sickness," a word that introduces some of the language and concepts used in this book. The medical anthropologist Arthur Kleinman, who has done an extensive comparative analysis of Chinese and U.S. medical systems, uses the term "sickness" to describe a "socially learned and sanctioned experience." A "disease," by contrast, is seen as "a malfunctioning in or maladaptation of the biological and/or psychological processes." "Illness" signifies the "experience of disease . . . and the societal reaction to disease."[3] In terms of these distinctions, Devia's infirmity would be considered a sickness according to his cultural and social norms, would be labeled a disease by doctors at the Hospital de Caridad, but would be experienced by Devia as an illness. Sickness is thus a part of both social and cultural systems that can be studied comparatively and across time. Significantly, in this way of thinking, a "disease [or a sickness] is not an entity but an explanatory model."[4] The manner by which a disease is explained, in combination with the knowledge that explains it, is known as framing. Frames of diseases differ over time and in different cultures.[5]

Devia sought relief from his infirmity within a medical system, "a patterned, interrelated body of values and deliberate practices, governed by a single paradigm of the meaning, identification, prevention, and treatment of sickness."[6] Medical systems combine technologies, knowledge, practitioners, institutions, and ideologies.[7] Devia noted as much in linking his illness with attempts to find a cure by visiting doctors and, finally, getting relief, for which he thanked Providence.

Medical systems integrate these—and other—variables into a unified whole. Understandings about diseases and illnesses constitute fundamental aspects of a culture, part of which is manifested within the medical system. Although distinct medical systems might share some characteristics, the contrasts among them are often so profound as to be untranslatable, fomenting misunderstandings and, quite frequently, extreme hostility among the practitioners of the different systems.

Healers

Healers are integral components of all medical systems. Most sicknesses are self-treated by the individual or members of her or his family,[8] but many others require the assistance of a healer who can diagnose and treat the illness. Although Perdomo was alternately labeled a *curandero*, an *empírico*, and a *médico*, these terms also had more specific meanings in his day. A *curandero* was a general healer, one who applied her or his skills to a variety of diseases or maladies. An *empírico*, or empiric, was not trained at a formal medical institution but had completed an apprenticeship with a lay healer. Formally trained healers were often referred to as *médicos*, a category that included the physicians at the Hospital de Caridad who criticized Perdomo.

A wide variety of healers exist within different medical systems; Devia, for example, apparently sought the assistance of several different types before visiting Perdomo. And, as Charles Rosenberg notes, "diagnosis and prognosis, the intellectual and social framing of disease, have always been central to the doctor-patient relationship."[9] Within some medical systems the frame of a disease is well known to patient and healer alike, although treatment might require specialized knowledge and abilities. In other instances the knowledge necessary to frame and treat a disease is held only by the healer and is unknown to the patient. These knowledge differences help to label healers and medical systems.

Virginia Gutiérrez de Pineda suggests that in Colombian popular medicine, the healer likely speaks the same language as the patient, shares the same culture, and uses herbs and technologies familiar to the patient. This pattern of common knowledge is generally characteristic of social medicine. It is less characteristic of the healer-patient relationship in professional medicine.[10] Social medicine, according to Laurel Ulrich, is scarcely visible as it operates through local networks of personal affiliation, whereas professional medicine seeks to distinguish itself from the communities that it serves through regional or cosmopolitan networks. Healer-patient differentiation is seen in the frequent use of titles, which are earned through professional and institutional training and sustained by licensure from legal authorities. By contrast, social healers acquire knowledge incrementally, through the "slow build-up of seemingly casual experience."[11] (Much of what is labeled social medicine is also referred to as household or domestic medicine, wherein the treatment of a disease is provided by members of the household.) Perdomo's approach was characteristic of social medicine. The *médicos* at the school of medicine clearly practiced professional medicine.

The characterization of *curanderos* in the border area of Mexico and the United States further illustrates the distinctions between social and professional medicine. As Robert Trotter II and Juan Antonio Chavira observe, "The curandero is often a person chosen from the community, who shares the same experiences, the same language, and the same socioeconomic status as his or her patients. The curandero is highly accessible, without the intervening variables of excessive social and spatial distance that sometimes affect the delivery of health [care] in the United States. Usually the only major distinctions between the curandero and the patient are the curandero's healing powers and medicinal knowledge."[12] Latin America *curanderos* are certainly social healers who, in addition to using "culturally appropriate methods of dealing with the patients," also employ "religious and spiritual aspects of the healing process." *Curanderos* tend not to secularize the process of healing as do rationalist, professional healers; their healing is not separated from the spiritual world of the person who is ill.[13] This holistic approach is characteristic of medical systems that are often labeled traditional.[14]

Trotter and Chavira indicate that *curanderos* employ different therapies on sick persons. The healer might engage in a specific medical therapy, as Perdomo did when he removed the tumor affecting Devia's eye, or else might perform a general procedure, a symbolic dimension of healing that could involve dance, song, interview, incantation, or some other ritual. There is an important analytical distinction between specific and general therapies, but the differences are constructed by observers who place more importance upon them than the healer or sick person might. Healing occurs because the sick person believes in the efficacy of the therapy and—often to a lesser extent—because the treatment is effective. Daniel E. Moerman suggests that between 35 and 60 percent of the effectiveness of medical intervention is rooted in the belief system of the culture—that is, in the "general medical therapy" or "placebo effect," not in the specific medical treatment.[15] For example, the rationalist understanding that dominates U.S. culture holds that the body responds to the laws of nature, laws that biomedical doctors largely understand and can therefore manipulate to effect a cure. Faith in a doctor's ability to mechanically correct a natural defect enhances the placebo effect.

Different types of medicine practiced by healers yield different amounts of historical documentation. Professional medicine is most visible in the historical record due to its institutional presence and the formal authority that it wields. Medical schools, bureaucratic organizations, policing agencies, professional associations, and titled doctors produce an abundance of documents for the historian's inquiries. Social medicine, which in Latin America is usually classified as popular or traditional medicine, appears most frequently in the historical record when it conflicts with professional medicine, when it runs afoul of public authority, or when it can be gleaned from documents produced for other purposes. Thus, commentators such as Isaac Holton, a visitor to Colombia in the 1850s, could reasonably state that 90 percent of the population received no medical assistance from birth until death.[16] His claim says nothing about the frequency of sickness or the utilization of healers; it says much about the invisibility of social medicine.

The identification of healers should be taken not as an indication of their relative presence in the past but as an insight into the social system that produced and maintained documents. Some observers are sensitive to the social context of healing. Friedrich Hassaurek, U.S. minister to Ecuador in the mid-1860s, commented that two-fifths of Quito's 40,000 inhabitants were Indians who "never submit to scientific medical treatment"; another 40 percent were *cholos* (mestizos) who were "too poor to pay a physician." The rest utilized scientific medicine, although its practitioners were reportedly few in number and often unskilled.[17] In late-twentieth-century Latin America, an estimated 70 to 80 percent of reported incidents of illness were treated (or not, as the case may be) outside the official, professional medical system that tends to produce more documentation.[18]

Knowledge

Identifying the sources of knowledge that frame disease further helps to distinguish medical systems. Healers in social or popular medical systems utilize common knowledge that is available to all. The knowledge of healers within professional medicine, by contrast, is specialized and sets these individuals apart. Perdomo noted as much when he commented, "And me . . . ignorant as I am, without having read one of your books, not knowing anything of this wisdom and science; me, a poor man of the people, challenged by you scientific eminences, can . . . do these things and more in surgery and in medicine, and I do have secrets."[19]

Knowledge in scientific medicine reflects a specialized access to nature obtained through training and methodologies that reveal the "incontrovertible" truths of that nature.[20] The *médicos* at the Hospital de Caridad suggested this in stating, "We don't want to place Mr. Perdomo in the obligation of having to undergo an examination, because we know beforehand that he is ignorant of the structure of the human body, that he knows nothing of the three realms of nature, and that the medical progress of the day are for him problems lost in the darkness of ignorance. We only ask, then, practical proofs, but in the light, without circumlocution or mystification."[21] The physicians sought to distance themselves from Perdomo, establish their dominion over the knowledge of nature, and make their professional status clear. For his part, Perdomo, "a poor man of the people," sought a social identity, even though his skills were enhanced by "secrets." The distancing employed by the professional doctors, in juxtaposition to the unity suggested by the *curandero*, does much to explain the social divisions evident in the 1872 disturbances in Bogotá.

Practitioners of distinct medical systems adhere to profoundly different ideologies, and each group tends to think of its own ideology as *the* truth. Seldom do members of one medical system acknowledge the possible validity of other truths. As a result, attitudes toward healers of another system are often highly negative. In their discussion of border *curanderos*, Trotter and Chavira suggest that criticisms of *curanderismo* generally originate in a simple "disbelief in the moral validity of the system," a rejection of sociocultural stereotypes associated with traditional practices, and a concern over the physical well-being of patients under the *curandero*'s care.[22] The criticisms of Perdomo appear to have similar bases.

For Devia and other patients who testified on Perdomo's behalf, knowledge and truth were less a concern than the accessibility, efficacy, and cost of healing. In a study of one Bolivian town, Libbet Crandon-Malamud has found that "cosmopolitan," Aymaran (Indian), and household medicines coexist within a system of medical pluralism. There, household medicine, which manifests both Aymaran and Hispanic folk characteristics, is likely to be the first treatment tried for an illness. Indigenous healers also treat Aymara people for a variety of afflictions. And an Aymara methodist would certainly seek assistance from the cosmopolitan hospital, as might someone who aspired to social mobility.[23] Medical pluralism exists in most of Latin America, even though some countries authorize scientific medicine as official. People who are sick tend to use one healer or another, depending upon many variables, including race, ethnicity, gender, class, ideology, and availability.

Medical systems are part of a broad cultural framework that encompasses social structures, institutions, and ideology. Medical knowledge is created through a historical process that, though often poorly understood, is essential for grasping the interplay among medical systems. Perdomo functioned as a healer within a colonial medical spectrum, an understanding of which requires an extended discussion of the medical systems of the Americas—the region known to the Spaniards as the Indies.

Precontact Medical Systems

The northern Andes region in which Perdomo operated was home to many different cultures prior to the Spanish Conquest. Toward the end of the fifteenth century the Inca Empire had been extended through Ecuador into what is today southern Colombia, subordinating the Pastos, Caras, Panzaleos, and other highland groups. (Lowland peoples were not effectively subjugated by the Incas.) Much of central Colombia fell under the loosely confederated Muisca polity, although certain groups, such as the Panches, fiercely resisted its control.[24] The Spaniards brought disease and colonialism, both of which exacted a heavy toll on the natives of Colombia and Ecuador, although indigenous cultures survived to a much greater extent in the latter country.[25] In Ecuador, indigenous leaders continued to exert considerable influence on Indian communities and culture, but their subordination to colonial rule was never in doubt.

Religious beliefs figured prominently in most indigenous medical systems. The lines between faith and specific healing remedies were blurred, much as they are in Catholic healing traditions, for the medical systems were rooted in an understanding of the spiritual world and the relationships among gods, the animate and physical worlds, and humans. Seldom could the spiritual world be interpreted by a layperson. What was required instead was the intervention of a specialist, called by many names but referred to as a "shaman" in this volume except where cited by a distinct name. Shamans served as repositories of community knowledge not only about healing but also about the relationship between society and beliefs.[26] In the Kingdom of Quito, many shamans used herbs such as tobacco or *huántu* (a native drug) in their healing techniques. Others breathed upon the patient directly or blew through a pipe to remove illness.[27] In most cultures a shaman could be either male or female, with apprentices chosen by heredity or by the revelation of a sign to the practicing healer.[28] Shamans often survived the conquest period as community leaders, attaining greater political importance than they had had during the preconquest period.[29]

Shamans certainly were not the only healers in indigenous medical systems, but the limited amount of information on preconquest practices prevents a detailed survey of the other types of healers treating patients in that era. Joseph Bastien's work on the contemporary Kallawaya people suggests that distinctions may have been made between spiritists, diviners, and herbalists, however. Spiritists, he notes, "cure with prayers that intercede with the powers of the sacred places or earth shrines . . . [by entering] a trance to negotiate an exchange with the dead so that, instead of taking the life of the sick person, the dead will be satisfied with the life of a chicken or llama."[30] Diviners, by contrast, "diagnose the causes of illness . . . and prepare elaborate rituals to feed the earth shrines. They are comparable to prophetic priests in Western religions. Like spiritists, diviners are qualified to the degree that they possess intuitive and diagnostic powers."[31] And herbalists "cure with plants, minerals, and animal products and are the traditional equivalents of modern-day pharmacists." Historically, Bastien adds, "diviners . . . concentrated on the spiritual, cosmological, and telluric dimensions of healing; and herbalists . . . dealt with empirical factors." Some healers blend these facets of healing, and others specialize in one of the functions,[32] but all attempt to locate the cause of illness and seek its cure within the context of the Kallawaya culture, presumably in manners akin to the practice of healers within earlier Andean medical systems.

Shamans approach the task of healing in ways that reflect their society's interaction with the natural world.[33] In their view, illnesses involve natural and supernatural forces that affect all people and that result from an imbalance or deviation from community or supernatural mores. Quite often, they believe, illness originates in the "magical" actions of one's enemies, necessitating the intervention of the shaman to ward off their influence.[34] People in areas that had been conquered by the Inca likely related illness and health to community well-being, whereas lowland peoples tended to associate the supernatural more directly with healing. Bastien suggests that highland hydraulic needs shaped a humoral understanding in which the unimpeded flow of fluids through the human body ensured health, just as water would sustain agricultural productivity. Blockages in the flow of these fluids were thought to result in illness. Treatment involved the use of chants, herbs, drugs, purgatives, and stylized cleansing rituals to restore a balance either within the patient's body or in the relationship between that body and the supernatural world.[35] Hispanic outsiders, who lacked the cultural knowledge with which to interpret healing rituals, often labeled them as magical or, more frequently, demonic.[36]

Indigenous influences persisted in the Ecuadorean highlands to a much greater extent than in any location in Colombia where it is documented that Perdomo practiced. Because the demographic and cultural presence of indigenous peoples quickly declined in much of highland Colombia, Hispanic social and cultural norms soon dominated most of the region, as they did in urban Ecuador. Given that the social context in which Perdomo operated appears to have been predominantly Hispanic, he likely incorporated fewer indigenous influences in his medical practices than might have been expected for a mestizo healer in highland Bolivia.

Even in regions where indigenous cultures remained strong, precontact beliefs and practices were resignified as the people were colonialized. Certain aspects of the medical system brought by the Spaniards were incorporated with ease. Humoral understandings, for example, paralleled Andean hydraulic concepts, and attitudes about the role of religious beliefs in the healing process were also compatible. This enabled pre-Hispanic medical culture to coexist with and often infiltrate colonial society. In many areas a large number of indigenous healers became *curanderos* who practiced among wide segments of the colonial populace.[37] Moreover, healers within the Hispanic system often sought out indigenous drugs and attempted to exploit their mystique as a part of the treatment.[38]

Precontact Hispanic Medicine

The medical system of late-fifteenth-century Spain featured a rich mixture of humoral, Christian, and Islamic influences. A thin veneer of academic medicine, supported by a limited institutional structure, covered the informal medical system under which most people lived. Because Spain was a former Roman colony, Hippocratic and Galenic beliefs underpinned the country's widespread acceptance of humoral understandings of disease. Through the Catholic Church came a deepseated belief in the role of the divine in healing. And Islamic influences appeared in the institutional structures of medicine—structures that reflected the growing influence of monarchical authority by the time of contact.

Spanish medical practices fit squarely within Western medical traditions in the fifteenth century, many of which had emerged in Greece at least five centuries before the birth of Christ. Humoral medicine is identified with Hippocrates of Cos (ca. 460–ca. 370 B.C.E.),[39] who asserted that illness stemmed from the imbalances of the humors, or fluids, of the human body. The body was envisioned to have four humors flowing through it: blood, phlegm, yellow bile or vomit, and black bile, the only humor not associated with a body product. According to this theory, food entered the digestive system through the stomach, where it would be separated into chyle and feces, and chyle then flowed into the liver, where it was cooked into the different humors. The humors continued to be transformed by cooking or fermentation as they moved through the body. The Greeks associated certain qualities with the four elements that made up the natural world: fire (hot), air (cold), earth (dry), and water (moist). And opposing pairs of these elemental qualities were linked with each humor: hot and moist with blood, cold and moist with phlegm, hot and dry with yellow bile, and cold and dry with black bile.[40]

Humoralists believed that good health required a humoral balance and that illness resulted from the production of morbid humors (for example, when too much food was consumed for the stomach to cook thoroughly). Morbid humors, they said, could be identified by taste, smell, or sight—the color of urine, a bad taste in the mouth, and so forth.[41] Food that purportedly had humoral qualities (for example, squash, cold and wet; cloves, hot and dry) and exercise served as the initial "regimen" to offset a humoral imbalance and restore health. If more direct intervention was needed, bloodletting, expectorants, plasters, salves, laxatives, diuretics, enemas, or purges were used to redress the imbalance of humoral fluids.[42] Careful study of particular prescriptions produced more efficacious cures for certain imbalances, and over time these prescriptions came to serve as the "recipe book" for humoral medicine, with hot medicines used to treat cold illnesses and dry medicines used for illnesses generated by excessive moisture. Humoral knowledge permeated Greek society and was not the privileged domain of physicians, although some people acquired more specialized healing skills. Scholars incorporated humoral knowledge in their texts and added it to a body of learning. Medical practitioners, by contrast, healed sufferers according to appropriate therapeutic practices.[43]

Like Hippocrates, Galen of Pergamum (ca.129–199 A.D.) had a long-term influence on Western medical beliefs. Galen not only helped to synthesize the corpus of Hellenic medical understanding into the Roman Empire, but he also added to it, especially in the realms of anatomy and physiology. As surgeon to the gladiators, he had abundant opportunities to study the body firsthand, making observations that he supplemented by dissecting various apes. His careful classification of diseases through case histories, observation, diagnosis, and prognosis filled the multiple volumes of his writings.[44]

The transformation of the Greco-Roman world into the Holy Roman Empire signaled that the locus of medical knowledge was shifting to the east as scientific inquiry declined in the Roman core. As will be discussed later, the Roman Empire increasingly came under the influence of Christian healing ideologies even as the corpus of the Hippocratic-Galenic knowledge base shifted eastward to Byzantium, where it was later revived and expanded by Islamic Syrian and Persian scholars. In fact, Hunayn ibn Ishaq (808–873) and others translated scores of Galenic works and many Hippocratic texts, and by the end of the millennium "almost the entire corpus of Greek medicine" had been translated into Arabic.[45]

The revival of European scholarly learning began on the frontiers of Christendom and Islam. Although some Christian religious communities had preserved limited Galenic and Hippocratic knowledge after the fall of Rome, the corpus of this medical knowledge had resided in Muslim lands.[46] The Benedictine monk Constantine the African, writing in the second half of the eleventh century, translated numerous Hippocratic and Galenic texts from Arabic into Latin. The *reconquista* (reconquest) of Toledo made the vast Moorish intellectual accomplishments available to the Christians, turning Spain into a seat of learning. Gerard of Cremona (ca. 1114–1187) translated the *Canon of Medicine*, written by Ibn Síná (also known as Avicenna, 980–1037), and numerous Galenic works, thereby opening the body of Greek and Islamic traditions to medieval universities.[47] Many sixteenth-century educational institutions, influenced by the new humanism of the Italian Renaissance, reintroduced Galenic texts into the medical curriculum, from whence they were eventually transferred to the Indies.

Medieval conceptions of disease were based on humoral theory but articulated in terms of a person's "complexion"—the balance of the four elements and their accompanying characteristics. One's body was believed to have four complexions that, when kept in balance, ensured good health. "Nonnaturals" such as air, food and drink, sleep, wakefulness, activity, rest, retention, and elimination, along with state of mind, were thought to influence disease, and healthiness was said to require the maintenance of balance by diet (since food served as the foundation for all humors) or through interventions such as bleeding or inducing vomiting. Drug therapy was the most common intervention, with folk drug prescriptions often used in academic medicine.[48]

Medicine in that and other eras had both academic and practical applications, although the boundaries between these applications were often blurred. Healers with formal education had little influence upon medical practices in areas such as surgery—a situation that at least partially stemmed from the fact that in 1130 the Council of Clermont had forbidden monks to practice surgery, thereby leading to the slow evolution of lay surgeons.[49] Barber-surgeons were often members of guilds. Empirics might perform surgery as well, but they had no formal or regulated training. Surgeons of that era were frequently disdained because surgery was considered a practice of last resort, filled with pain and little hope of relief. Some surgeons had limited formal education but acquired more of their skills through experience. Most were lay surgeons—barbers or bleeders—who attended to a majority of the population.

These aforementioned methods of treatment dominated Western medical practice at the time of contact, and they were propagated through a variety of mechanisms, including medical education, hospitals and missionary orders, *recetarios* (recipe books or home medical guides), pharmacies, and social custom, with the latter being the most influential. As will be seen, the Church, more than any other institution, diffused Hispanic medical practices and conceptions of healing throughout Latin America. Importantly, medical practices and belief systems remained largely integrated with religious thought—a unity of great significance in the case of Miguel Perdomo Neira.

Christianity and Healing

The Church occupied a central role in Hispanic medical institutions and healing ideologies. A letter from the "poor and indigent" of Guaduas in praise of Perdomo declared that "charity is the fundamental foundation of Christianity,"[50] clearly reflecting Catholic doctrine, which insists that charity, the first of the Christian virtues, surpasses even moral virtues.[51] Jesus Christ used healing as a form of charity on many occasions; and from its inception, Christianity depicted itself as a healing faith.[52] Through its selfless production of social good, true charity was seen to demonstrate the love of God in the simple act of helping others. In establishing early Christian doctrines, Paul of Tarsus drew upon these tenets to make charity a cornerstone of Christian ethics. And early monasteries demonstrated charitable works in hospices and hospitals for the needy.[53]

From the time of the conversion of the Roman state to Christianity, the Church had positioned itself among the regulators of the medical professions. Christian ideology emphasized compassion and caring for the sick, traits that were often manifested in some form of hospital care. Monastic orders took in the sick but did little to treat them, believing that God would either see to the patients' recovery or death. Appeals could certainly be made to God, usually through the intermediary of a saint or holy person. And as illness came to be associated with the influence of evil or the devil, people increasingly turned to prayer or sought religious intercession. Priests necessarily took over much of this responsibility, and they began to assume a significant role in medical practice after the fall of Rome. However, because the Christian church viewed care of the soul as far more important than care of the body, medical treatment and even physical cleanliness were little valued; mortification of the flesh was even seen as a sign of saintliness. Nearly all Europeans eventually came to look upon illness as a condition caused by supernatural forces, perhaps in the form of diabolical possession. Hence, religious means were among the primary healing treatments of that age. Every malady had a patron saint to whom prayers were directed by the patient, family, friends, and the community. Particular saints were believed to intercede on behalf of the ill: Saint Niçaise for smallpox, Saint Blaise for respiratory disease, and Saint Roch for the plague.

The depiction of illness in association with humankind's fall from grace complemented remnant Greek knowledge by the medieval period. Clerics actively participated in all aspects of the healing professions through the early thirteenth century. By the fourteenth century, as the universities became the centers of medical learning, the Church seemed content to assist in regulating them for the common good, rather than directing medical education itself.[54] Faith in the healing power of God served as the foundation for most popular European healing ideologies.

The relationship between healers and sainthood is common to the Mediterranean cultural area, which includes Latin America.[55] Although most early saints were martyrs, charitable works earned a plurality of medieval saints their status. Wonder-working took the form of miraculous healing, raising the dead, or comforting the sick.[56] The *potentia* (potency) of the saint was thought to persist in her or his shrine, and many reverential pilgrimages were undertaken to search for healing.[57] In addition to persons canonized by the Church, "visible saints"—or folk saints—are revered throughout the Mediterranean cultural area as "models of and for life and social action." At times, these visible saints have been canonized; more often, they are accorded social power outside the bounds of the formal Church structure.[58]

Perdomo operated within this Catholic framework of healing. While many testimonials about Perdomo speak of "miraculous cures," at no time did he claim to possess supernatural abilities. He attributed his knowledge to experience and to the acquisition of "certain plants from the vegetable kingdom" that enabled him to operate and undertake healing therapeutics. Although those plants might have been unknown to science, he saw them as a "special favor from Heaven, accorded by God to a poor and humble man of the people."[59] Perdomo reportedly observed a triduum and other religious rituals upon his arrival in a town. One Bogotano commented that the healer's table held medicine, surgical instruments, and an oil painting of the Sacred Heart of Jesus, and José María Cordovez Moure related that Perdomo prayed to the image prior to his healing, seeking divine assistance for his cures. Although this liberal commentator added that "I didn't need anything else to help me form an opinion of that hypocrite,"[60] such rituals clearly sustained popular healing ideologies informed by Catholic traditions. It is quite likely that many people viewed the *curandero* as a visible saint for his service to the ill in the name of charity.

Perdomo's relationship to Catholic healing tradition is also reflected in the name of his hacienda—San Juan de Dios. San Juan de Dios is the patron saint of the ill and of hospitals, and the fundamental relationship between the Church, charity, and healing is illustrated in the story of his life. Juan Ciudad Suárez (1495–1550), a Portuguese soldier who fought with Spain against the Moors in northern Africa, experienced a profound revelation in a military hospital in Granada in 1539. Military hospitals had served the poor for hundreds of years, notably under the Order of Hospitallers, the Knights of Saint John of Jerusalem.[61] Shortly before the First Crusade, several monks founded a hospice for pilgrims in Jerusalem, which became a military hospital during the armed struggle of the Crusades. Hospices were established in other areas of religious conflict throughout the Mediterranean, all of which linked service to the Crusaders and the poor;[62] some of these hospitals also aided Christians in the reconquest of the Iberian Peninsula from the Moors. Ciudad committed himself to the service of God by providing hospital care to the military and the poor in Granada. After his death in 1550, several of his followers expanded his labors, organizing hospitals in numerous Spanish towns and thereby earning themselves the status of a congregation in 1571. Pope Innocent XII canonized Ciudad as Juan de Dios in 1691, conferring on him the status of spiritual benefactor of the Brothers of the Order of Hospitallers of Saint John of God.[63]

The order proved to be a powerful institutional force in the northern Andes and other areas of the Indies. King Philip II granted members of the order permission to undertake a medical mission in the Indies in 1595, directing that they begin in the Provinces of Cartagena, Nombre de Dios, and Panama. Within a generation the order had founded hospitals in most major towns of the realm,[64] and by 1700 almost sixty hospitals had been established. As in Spain, the order dedicated its initial energies to military hospitals, but the paucity of other medical institutions meant that San Juan de Dios hospitals were often the only institutionalized medical facilities available to townspeople, just as they were in Spain. In addition, physicians at the hospitals engaged in educational activities, training individuals who later worked as lay surgeons or empirics.[65] San Juan de Dios hospitals appeared in Bogotá, Quito, Guayaquil, Popayán, Cali, and dozens of other towns in New Granada. Although the precise relationship between Perdomo and the San Juan de Dios hospitals is unclear, the hospital at his hacienda and the order itself clearly had the same healing mission.

By 1500 humoral and Catholic medical beliefs were joined into a largely integrated medical system. As Patricia Vila de Pineda writes, contact-era Spain practiced a "magical religious medicine." In Spain, "psalms, prayers, *reliquias* [relics], [and] images of saints are mixed with purgatives, bleeding, diets, the principles of hot and cold humors, and in the most simple cases with drugs."[66] These medical practices were undoubtedly understood by most Spaniards, which suggests that they had a social character, but they did not constitute the central features of the formal medical system.

Spanish Medical Institutions

The state, the municipality, and the university complemented the Church in the formalized Hispanic medical system. The 1469 marriage of Isabella of the Kingdom of Castile and Ferdinand of Aragón signaled the centralization of monarchical authority on the Iberian Peninsula. Within ten years, Isabella and Ferdinand had become monarchs of their respective kingdoms, thereby consolidating their crowns into a single dynastic line. With this consolidation came an increased capacity to centralize the formal medical system, although centralization never extinguished the authority of municipalities to direct local affairs. Nor did it significantly alter the role of the Church in healing.[67]

The final stages of the *reconquista* led to the establishment of the *protomedicato*, an institution charged with the regulation of official healing practices and the management of public health. (*Protomedicato* also denotes the officer of that institution.) In 1477 the "king's physicians" were empowered by Ferdinand and Isabella to "examine all who aspired to become physicians, surgeons, bone setters, apothecaries, dealers in aromatic drugs, [and] herbalists," as well as all those who practiced these trades "in whole or in part."[68] *Protomedicatos* regulated local medical services such as the *botica* (a multipurpose drugstore) and assisted municipalities in sanitary and public health concerns.[69] They attempted, not always with success, to limit the numbers of unofficial practitioners,[70] a task that would prove to be more complicated in the Indies. In Spain the *protomedicato* came to be a powerful instrument of state authority, but in the Indies, municipalities tended to have more influence over this body than did the crown.

The *protomedicato* assisted in coordinating the supervision of formalized medicine. This was especially the case within the notable institutions of higher education, particularly the universities of

Salamanca, Aragón, Alcalá de Henares, and Santiago de Compostela. Spanish medical ideology as taught in the universities drew upon Hippocratic and Galenic understandings interpreted through Muslim intermediaries, especially Avicenna. The Universidad de Salamanca, for example, adopted Muslim traditions in its development of a medical curriculum that, after being formalized in 1561, would dominate both Spanish and colonial higher education until the nineteenth century. It dictated that the prima chair would utilize the texts of Avicenna for the first three years of study, and the vísperas chair would teach Hippocrates and Galen. Students learned through the scholastic method, which left little room for either professorial flexibility or student creativity. This emphasis upon theory and texts was supplemented by limited clinical exposure, especially in dissection and anatomy.[71] Surgeons often trained at Church-administered hospitals, including that of the Monastery of Guadalupe.[72]

Once in place, this medical system changed very slowly. Innovations in surgical preparation at the general hospital in Madrid and in Cadiz during the 1740s heralded significant reforms. Charles III regularized the preparation of physicians in 1771, establishing a norm of six chairs—prima, vísperas, prognosisi, method, surgery, and anatomy.[73] French physicians helped introduce the work of Hermann Boerhaave and other new medical currents, a process that accelerated during the Napoleonic Wars,[74] leading to the nineteenth-century transformation of the Spanish medical system.

Hispanic healers can be stratified by the sources of their knowledge. Only the elite of the formal Hispanic medical hierarchy had institutionalized training. Such physicians received a university education, with limited experiential preparation. Physicians with a doctoral degree and an approved title occupied the highest echelon and generally taught in the universities. "Latin surgeons"—those who had some university preparation but had not completed their studies—occupied the next rung. Apprenticed "Romance surgeons," often trained by Latin surgeons in hospitals but lacking university preparation, completed the category of professional healers.[75] Many of Perdomo's medical skills were practiced by so-called surgeons during the colonial period. Colonial surgeons might have trained for up to five years with approved surgeons, or they might have been empirics who operated with somewhat less training and less social prestige.[76] Similarly, Perdomo may well have trained with a professional or with another empiric; no evidence suggests how he acquired his surgical knowledge.

These physicians and surgeons constituted only a small percentage of the healers of the age. Most healers were empirics who specialized in particular skills and medical procedures, such as bleeding (*barbero*) or childbirth (*partera*). Experiential learning was crucial to an empiric's knowledge, which was more similar to that of the social (not professional) healer. Some empirics were at the boundary between social and professional medicine, although most undoubtedly fit comfortably within the social category and are consequently absent from the historical record. A third category consisted of magical healers, astrologers, or necromantic conjurers.[77]

Hispanic Medical Institutions in the Indies

The formalized system of Hispanic medicine in the Indies developed parallel to that in Spain. The institution of the *protomedicato* crossed the Atlantic in the 1520s, albeit with significant modifications. The municipal council of Mexico City established the first *protomedicato* in New Spain in 1525; the council in Lima did the same twelve years later. City councils in the Indies generally replaced the crown in terms of supporting medical institutions. Municipal councils also played an active role in the establishment and regulation of medical professions, a role constantly plagued by an acute shortage of trained physicians, a scarcity of funds, and tensions among elite factions. Because the colonial *protomedicatos* faced the awesome task of overseeing colonial medical practices in widely varied urban settings, the medical institutions of each city took on a distinct character.[78] Institutional Hispanic medicine can be seen as the official medicine, in that public authorities promulgated a particular medical system through its authority.

The Hispanic medical system in the Indies filtered down to the general populace from centers of learning, through elite practitioners, through religious orders, and through informal social networks. The filtration process followed at least five recognizable routes: universities, hospitals, missionary orders, pharmacies, and home medical guides.[79] Priests taught medical theory at Mexico City's Colegio de Tlatelolco in the 1530s, although formal medical education was not set up until the late 1570s with the establishment of the prima chair at the Real y Pontífica Universidad de México. The vísperas chair was added in 1599. A medical chair was established at the Universidad de San Marcos in Lima, Peru, in 1634, followed by a chair in the "method of Galen" in 1690. Just as in Spain, texts by Hippocrates, Galen, and Avicenna dominated the curricula until the early national period.[80] In these and other institutions of higher education, soon-to-be physicians and other members of the elite were exposed to a common medical ideology based upon Galenic theory.

Religious orders established most hospitals in the Indies and often treated patients as a part of their charitable ministry. A hospital was founded in Mexico City in 1522, although not until some ten years later did the crown intervene with the opening of two hospitals in the viceregal capital, one for *indios* (Indians) and one for *blancos* (Spaniards). The Mexican Council of 1555 directed the Church to set up a hospital in every town, an ambitious goal pursued by the Mendicant orders;[81] more than 150 were in operation in New Spain by the end of the sixteenth century. The Brothers of the Charity of Saint Hippolytus, the Bethlemites, the Jesuits, and San Juan de Dios were the most active orders and helped to found lay confraternities (*cofradías*) that served as hospital associations for the indigenous and mestizo populations.[82] Formal healing was primarily accessible to most non-Spanish patients through the hospitals—institutions through which Spanish medical ideologies could be inculcated into the general populace. These hospitals were usually supported by both Church funds and gifts made to religious groups.[83]

City councils throughout the Indies used the *protomedicato* to provide public health services. A council's responsibilities included tending to the health of the city dwellers, a responsibility that placed the municipal council directly in the middle of all disputes involving health care delivery. Cities usually had a "public doctor" hired by the council, even though the delivery of health services varied widely and was limited by funds and the availability of physicians. Those hired by the municipal council generally served in the hospitals, dividing their time between charitable and private practices. Quite often the shortage of trained physicians and Latin surgeons meant that there was considerable business for empirics, an outcome that *protomedicatos*, city councils, and trained physicians sought—generally in vain—to curtail. The pressing need for such services enabled some empirics to ascend the medical hierarchy, sometimes with the council's support, in return for assisting the community and the poor.[84]

Guides to home remedies and the pharmaceutical system further diffused Spanish medical techniques into colonial society. Home medical guides were printed in the Indies by the late sixteenth century and circulated throughout the empire. Typically, a guide would include a section on anatomy, descriptions of physical ailments, and a list of prescriptions, all of which drew upon Galenic principles. Some, most notably the *Suma y recopilación de cirugía* of Alonso López de Hinojosos, described indigenous herbs, analyzed for their humoral qualities, as well as those of the European pharmacy.[85] Physicians, empirics, clerics, hacendados, and others utilized these guides to treat illnesses. Many of the ingredients prescribed in the home medical guides could be found in the urban pharmacies, for *boticas* maintained the drugs, herbs, and medical supplies used by lay and professional healers (albeit with inevitable discrepancies in terms of quality and range of services). Where the *protomedicato* functioned well, *boticas* were supervised, but in most cases, they were not. The *botica* came to be a mainstay of local healing institutions.[86]

Indigenous Healing Influences on the Colonial Medical Spectrum

As Spanish medical practices filtered down into a rapidly changing ethnic world, indigenous systems largely remained intact and slowly filtered up to the world of the mestizos. Suzanne Alchon suggests that colonialism changed the indigenous medical ideologies in a significant manner, despite the fact that "healing practices changed very little."[87] The conquest of native gods upset the equilibrium that sustained native healing systems, a process exacerbated by Spanish efforts to purge idolatry from the Indies. Over time many indigenous peoples incorporated the idea of Satan as a cause of illness into their medical systems, a belief that gradually offset earlier sources of imbalance.[88] Traditional religious practices were frequently forced underground, or "behind altars," taking indigenous medical systems offstage.

The limited number of Spanish physicians treated only a small percentage of the urban population. Therefore, empirics and *curanderos* were the most prominent healers, despite sporadic efforts to limit their practices. These healers came to constitute something of an artisan guild in larger towns. They combined elements of popular and professional medicine and passed down their healing traditions, which drew upon both humoral and astrological beliefs and involved treatment with herbs, amulets, and bleeding.[89] In the countryside, where almost 95 percent of the population lived, access to a trained physician was rare or nonexistent. *Curanderos* and shamans predominated, for even empirics seldom ventured into rural areas. Healers in the countryside thus "assumed an importance beyond furnishing health care to the vast majority of rural poor. In fact, by preserving religious and social values, the *curandero* became an essential figure in the survival of traditional native culture. The use of magical procedures in healing helped native populations to maintain their identity and distinctiveness."[90]

Imperial dictates excluded those of "impure" blood or of Indian ancestry from the formal practice of medicine, thereby significantly reducing the potential pool of official healers. As a result, indigenous healers or those who borrowed from both native and Hispanic healing traditions were denied recognition. Although Hernán Cortés and others of the conquest generation expressed admiration for native healers, Spanish physicians came to look upon their practices with disdain. This tendency became quite pronounced by the beginning of the seventeenth century, as colonial institutions and physicians became more firmly entrenched. The *protomedicato* of New Spain, for example, declared in 1646 that only those with university degrees could legally practice medicine, in essence drawing a line between the limited number of Spanish physicians and the mass of Romance surgeons, empirics, *curanderos*, and shamans.[91] In New Spain and elsewhere the Inquisition investigated *curanderos* and lay healers, although evidence suggests that the Holy Office tacitly accepted the treatment of non-Spanish colonists by *curanderos*, preserving for titled physicians the privilege of treating Spaniards. Noemí Quezada suggests that this tolerance allowed for the "continuity of traditionalist medicine," which "syncretized Indian, black, and Spanish folk medicines."[92]

Protomedicatos often sought the assistance of non-Spaniards in the effort to provide health care to the Hispanic populace. Juan de Arias, the *protomedicato* of Cartagena, requested permission in 1805 to grant *zambos* (persons of indigenous and African ancestry) and mulattoes the right to practice medicine without a title. Arias lamented the lack of physicians and suggested that this move was a necessary remedy to that problem. The government denied the request, insisting that existing laws had to be obeyed.[93] People of color served as healers, but they did so without the legal sanction of the state—a restatement of the bifurcation between practice and law.

Empirics, *curanderos*, and other lay healers helped to solve Latin America's chronic problem of a shortage of professional doctors. As mentioned, residents of major imperial towns benefited from the services of trained physicians (at least white inhabitants did), but most small-town and rural dwellers had no access to such healers. John Tate Lanning describes vast stretches of Spanish America, such as 1812 Puerto Rico, where "hardly a single practitioner of surgery or medicine [practiced] throughout the length and breadth of the island."[94] The presidency of Quito complained that major cities had only a few trained physicians and that most areas had none at all. To bridge the gap, friars with some medical knowledge frequently ministered to the physical as well as the spiritual health of their parishioners. Many empirics apparently learned their trade by their observations at hospitals or at the sides of other empirics. Although the vast *gremio* (guild) of *curanderos* and *curanderas* was mentioned in historical records only when Latin physicians brought legal action against them,[95] most people turned to empirics, *curanderos*, and similar healers—not to the university graduates—for treatment of their illnesses.

Medical Institutions in Colonial New Granada

Medical services in the area of colonial New Granada that would become Colombia suffered from the poverty and relative isolation of the region. In most places, clerics, shamans, or lay healers delivered the bulk of the medical services. Only in towns such as Bogotá, Cartagena, Popayán, or Santa Marta did formalized medicine exist, and even Bogotá's medical services were less well organized than those of Mexico City or Lima. Not until the 1580s did the first titled physician, Alvaro de Auñón, arrive in Bogotá. Though *protomedicatos* were established in the viceregal capitals within ten years of conquest, none existed in Bogotá until Diego Henríquez arrived in 1639, more than a century after the town's founding. Henríquez carried out the standard functions of the office, examining medical students, granting licenses, overseeing pharmacies, and delivering medical instruction as chair of medicine at the Universidad del Convento de Santo Domingo. His office was filled sporadically after his death until the 1750s. In 1758, José Vicente Román Cancino, who had been practicing medicine in the capital for two decades, assumed the title of *protomedicato*. From then on, the position was filled more continuously.[96]

In the absence of a *protomedicato*, the Church and its universities served as the keystones of Bogotá's medical institutions. Juan de Barrios y Toledo, the town's first archbishop, established the Hospital de San Pedro in 1564 in two houses behind the cathedral. This facility was supported by Church funds and by money appropriated by the colonial state, but neither source of funding was very secure, so the institution was in constant need.[97] Smaller hospitals in other towns relied upon the same funding sources and confronted similar problems. In the face of epidemics, such as that of 1587, Archbishop Luis Zapata and other clerics organized and funded relief and medical services.[98] Clerical authorities appointed physicians in the absence of a *protomedicato*, and most clerics served the poor and destitute as part of their charitable mission. San Pedro was taken over by the Order of San Juan de Dios in 1635, becoming the Hospital de San Juan de Dios. At the time of the transfer the hospital had a total of thirty beds, twenty for men and ten for women.[99] Not until the late seventeenth century did comparable facilities become available in provincial towns such as Pasto, Cali, or Medellín.

Bogotá's poorly organized educational system prepared few medical students at its several seminaries and universities. The Jesuit order founded the Colegio de San Bartolomé in 1602. The Jesuits had organized the city's *botica* soon after their arrival, and they apparently regulated pharmaceuticals in the absence of a permanent *protomedicato*.[100] Systematized medical studies did not begin until the 1640s at the Dominicans' Universidad de Santo Domingo and in 1653 at the Colegio Mayor de Nuestra Señora del Rosario. These institutions did not, however, produce a corpus of titled physicians or Latin surgeons. In fact, only two physicians were granted medical titles between 1636 and 1802,[101] leaving the responsibility for healing in the hands of Romance surgeons, empirics, *curanderos*, and shamans. Clerics delivered health care at the hospital and in the convents and monasteries. A few Bogotanos, such as Francisco Díaz, earned their medical degrees in Spain before returning home to practice in Bogotá,[102] and immigrant physicians, such as Alvaro de Auñón, served the "nobility and clergy."[103] Pedro Ibáñez, who practiced medicine in the Colombian capital in the 1880s, noted that members of the informal empirics' guild "have been until these days charged with the practice of simple, minor surgery, which they offer in their respective professions to the poor and indigent of the city without charge."[104]

The San Juan de Dios order began constructing a new hospital in the viceregal capital in 1720s (it was completed in 1739), signaling a quickening pace of change in medical institutions.[105] After the expulsion of the Jesuits in 1767, the hospital assumed responsibility for both the Jesuits' *botica* and their house of foundlings. Father Miguel de Isla took charge of the hospital in the early 1780s, a time when considerable efforts were being made to coordinate the training of physicians, a process that will be described in Chapter 2.

Colonial Ecuador

Ecuador's system of formal medicine developed along a somewhat different trajectory. In contrast to Colombia, where indigenous populations declined precipitously and had relatively little effect upon colonial healing traditions, Ecuador's native population had strongly influenced the development of colonial medicine in both rural and urban settings. As in Colombia, the *protomedicato* operated only sporadically. The Church proved to be the most significant institutional force, supported in Quito and Guayaquil by the municipal council, an agency that was more influential there than in Colombia.[106]

As these colonial institutions defined the arena of public health, Hispanic physicians, empirics, *curanderos*, and shamans ministered to the needs of the private sector. Nicolás Larco Noboa notes that *curanderos* "were consulted more than titled surgeons, not only among Indians and rural peoples, but in all of our cities."[107] Few titled physicians established themselves permanently in the capital or elsewhere in the country, so that a *protomedicato* did not function until 1768. In its absence, the *cabildo* (municipal council) regulated medical practices and granted titles. Among its other actions the council appointed Fernando Meneses as a physician of the poor in the early seventeenth century, although he left for Lima shortly thereafter.[108]

Hispanic medical ideology, along with concerns about epidemic disease, shaped Ecuador's early colonial history. The *cabildo* issued a variety of edicts intended to ensure public health in the first years after conquest. An epidemic in 1546 led to the founding of the first hospital (Nuestra Señora de la Antigua), though it survived only a few years.[109] Religious hospitals provided important medical services, but only in major centers of population such as Quito, where the Hospital de Misericordia (1565) existed as an early example of the Church's medical services. Unfortunately, the hospital depended almost entirely upon gifts, and it closed periodically until being destroyed by fire in 1636. Shortly after the facility was reconstructed in 1693, the Bethlemite order took control of it, turning it into a charity hospital. In addition to the doctors and surgeons associated with the hospital, many members of the clergy engaged in healing as part of their ministry,[110] often through confraternities such as the Cofradía y Hermandad de la Caridad y Misericordia.[111]

The Church had a powerful medical presence through its hospitals and universities. Several religious orders established universities with medical privileges, including the Jesuits' Universidad de San

Gregorio Magno (1620) and the Dominicans' Universidad de Santo Tomás (1682). A chair of medicine was organized as a result of a royal *cedula* (edict) in 1693, and shortly thereafter, Santo Tomás began granting medical degrees. These schools enrolled only a handful of students because chairs were vacant more often than not, chiefly due to a lack of qualified physicians. The San Juan de Dios hospital, established in the early years of the eighteenth century, emerged as the single most important medical institution in Quito.[112]

Neither municipal nor ecclesiastical authorities succeeded in extending the Hispanic medical system much beyond the whites of Quito. A permanent shortage of funds plagued the *cabildo*. Since physicians relied upon the patronage of wealthy Hispanics and contractual relations with the *cabildo* to deliver public health, the sources of revenue proved insufficient to attract and maintain physicians.[113] Thus, while the local bishop attempted to fill this need through the services of the Church, "local officials and encomenderos were able to block the proposal [to bring in the San Juan de Dios hospital], and control remained in local hands until the eighteenth century."[114] *Cabildo* regulations prohibited the practice of medicine, pharmacy, or surgery without its approval, but, again, these statutes had little effect on the numbers of lay healers.

Late Colonial Healers

Few healers attracted the attention of those who documented the colonial era,[115] and of the limited number of healers who have been the subject of scholarly examination, only the briefest of information is known. An author known as "Shaman" related that popular doctors in Ecuador ranged from *curanderos* to *barberos*, *algebristas* (bonesetters), *herbolarios* (herbalists), and *parteros*, and quite often the *barberos* or *algebristas* were associated with the town's hospitals, thereby enhancing the religious influence upon healing.[116] Pedro Guerro, *El doctor Gallinazo*, was an Indian from Quito who developed a reputation as a highly skilled botanist and healer in the 1740s. He apparently specialized in the flora of the lowlands around Guayaquil, about which he wrote a monograph.[117] Other healers, such as José María Upegui ("don Chepe"), a surgeon in Antioquia, used bleeding, purgatives, and laxatives as their fundamental therapies. Don Chepe, who apparently had no formal training, engaged in a wide variety of surgical practices, including the extraction of molars, the removal of tumors, and the amputation of arms and legs.[118] The midwife Melchora, who was widely respected in the late colonial period, became a *curandera*. Her therapy included haircuts, cold baths, and the treatment of "internal crises" with doses of *agua de pollo* (literally, "chicken water").[119] José Hilario Cifuentes, a barber and bleeder, became the *peluquero* (barber) to both Simón Bolívar and Francisco de Paula Santander. He worked closely with the doctors and the Hospital de Caridad, especially during the epidemic of 1825, when he bled and scarred the ill as prescribed by the medical faculty. Manuel Coronado, from Quito, apparently learned to read and developed his skills while working with a member of the clergy. As an adult, he studied surgery and was admitted to the faculty of medicine, where he rose to the status of *maestro mayor* (senior teacher). Coronado, unlike many of his creole counterparts, attended to all social classes and cultures of patients.[120] This attitude was not shared by all nineteenth-century physicians.

Humoral medicine was deeply rooted in the Hispanic tradition, having evolved over hundreds of years before contact with the Indies. Many scholars contend that humoral medicine as it shaped Latin American medical systems originated in the Old World, whereas others argue for a separate indigenous origin that shaped Hispanic popular medicine.[121] Whatever the correct interpretation, evidence for the early presence of humoralism in Latin America comes from many sources. For example, in 1584, Licenciado de Monzón is reported to have died while being bled, a humoral treatment for excessive heat in the body.[122] A traveler to Ecuador in the mid-nineteenth century commented that many Hispanics had an aversion to cold water, in that they feared that it would cool internal organs and bring on certain types of illness.[123] And in his comments on the common method of diagnosis in the late colonial era, a nineteenth-century physician from Medellín related that examination of the color and smell of urine was crucial. A healer might also ask if the patient had a crust or film upon the tongue. Was saliva abundant or scarce? Was the person thirsty? Did he or she have heat (a fever)? These were all humoral methods of diagnosis.[124]

The case of Domingo Rota, a Romance surgeon with both practical and theoretical training, illustrates the depth of the humoral tradition in Latin America. Rota was born in Bogotá in 1752, where he had the opportunity to study grammar, Latin, and theology. In 1770 he worked as a silversmith but continued his connection with the Church, serving as the manager for a cathedral's tower clock. The healing function of the clerics soon captured his interest, however, and he slowly developed his medical skills. In *Casos felices y auténticos de medicina* (1830), which gives unique insight into colonial medical practices, Rota stated that he cured by using "simple" medical procedures. He practiced bleeding, used a variety of purgatives and wet plasters (treated with wine and soap, *aguardiente* [cane liquor], or water and milk), and relied upon dietary restrictions in his cures. His treatment methodology appears to have been completely humoral in nature, undoubtedly reflecting the practices of those clerics who instructed him.[125]

Some scientific doctors expressed an appreciation for the empirics of the colonial medical spectrum. Manuel Uribe Angel, who graduated from the Universidad Central de Bogotá in 1846 but practiced medicine in Medellín, is one example. He noted that although empirics administered prescriptions without rules or principles, they relied upon experience and the observation of their treatments with real success. "These physicians took full advantage of the botanical store of our rich tropical flora. They did not reach the full professional stature of the wise men of today. Their nomenclature was far from scientific; their knowledge was not based on scientific analysis; their qualifications were vulgar; and the virtues of plants were known to them by empirical tradition rather than by another route."[126] Still, most empirics were well-meaning and provided a valuable social good, one that Uribe called a "service to humanity."[127] Empirics and *curanderos* had a social function, taking an approach to healing that, though criticized by more professional and scientific doctors of the nineteenth century, was part of the colonial medical spectrum and familiar to the person needing medical assistance. Perdomo can be placed firmly within that medical system—a system of beliefs that was challenged over the course of the nineteenth century.

The Colonial Medical Spectrum

The colonization of the Americas by the Spaniards created a multifaceted medical spectrum dominated by Hispanic medicine, with countless indigenous medical systems occupying subordinate positions. Although Spanish law and high culture defined an "idealized" medical system, medicine in the Iberian Peninsula had long been pluralist in practice. In the newly conquered Indies, a complex mosaic of indigenous medical systems existed, roughly correlated to dominant cultural groups. These cultural patterns persisted into the colonial period, albeit in reduced and less prominent positions. People from Africa who were forced into slavery in the Americas took their own medical beliefs to the New World, making colonial medicine even more pluralist. The historical debility of the Spanish state prevented the development of an authoritarian medical system in the Indies, making medical pluralism more ethnocultural than legal. Time, cultural miscegenation, and changes in medical ideologies slowly blurred the boundaries. Under colonial conditions, the degree of indigenous cultural autonomy or miscegenation influenced the persistence of preconquest medical systems. My own sense is that, over time, these multiple medical systems combined to shape a colonial medical spectrum that represented the interaction of and, at times, the fusion of Hispanic, African, and indigenous medicines by the nineteenth century. Within that spectrum, Hispanic medicine was the dominant influence.

The introduction of rationalist, scientific medicine over the course of the nineteenth century usurped the authority of Hispanic medicine within the colonial medical spectrum. Scientific medicine took its authority from a claim to represent the natural world—a world whose characteristics could be revealed by scientific investigation. Significantly, practitioners of scientific medicine rejected other medical beliefs as inferior or, more often, primitive and inaccurate. The clashes that surrounded Perdomo reveal the different truth claims of the era.

2

"Science . . . Which Is
the Truth"

The intellectual framework that had sustained Western medical ideologies for hundreds of years came under considerable scrutiny beginning in the sixteenth century. The Church as the agent of God on Earth had reigned as the dominant source of authority for centuries, but rationalism provided another source from which new ideologies emerged. Just as René Descartes's succinct phrase "I think, therefore I am" spoke to this new authority, Cartesian dualism separated the rational mind and the physical body, dividing into separate fields what the Church had theretofore united. Humans created knowledge as they investigated the laws of the natural world that could be discovered by inquiring minds. The spirit of rationalism sustained the Enlightenment, an era of inquiry that produced an enormous corpus of knowledge that strengthened the new voice of authority's capacity to define the latest understandings of the world. Rationalism accompanied and helped to transform much of Europe into modern societies.

Colombian thinkers used rationalist logic to critique both the ideology and the methods of Perdomo. Writing in the 1880s, Medardo Rivas found incredible the claim that Perdomo could somehow discover fundamental medical "secrets" without the benefit of proper scientific investigation:

> The road of science advances only by degrees; it is impossible that one man could, by the singular force of his will, even though he might be favored in this task by admirable intellectual abilities, in a day travel these

distances, covering the terrain that humanity has traveled in centuries in a journey directed by luminaries, and by the discoveries of genius and study; it is impossible that one man, surrounded by the barriers that nature has imposed upon the human spirit, in one day arrives at the end and finds himself possessing all of the science known by humanity; and more, a science until then unknown and held as legendary among men.[1]

Rivas believed that progress could only come in methodical stages, with one generation building upon the knowledge of its predecessors. This "progressive" view of knowledge acquisition denied the capacity for revelation—or religious mysticism, in Rivas's estimation. Rivas and others like him simply doubted that Perdomo could have acquired the skills that he said he possessed without having a rational, scientific education: Only through education and experimentation could scientific medicine and many other areas of knowledge unearth the truths of the natural world. Such claims to knowledge about rational truth sustained the critics of Perdomo.

Rationalism and Medical Knowledge

This new conception of the natural order transformed knowledge and the practice of medicine. The Copernican revolution, in conjunction with the conceptions of Galileo, shifted the center of the cosmos away from the Earth, envisioning a cosmological order defined not by God but by awesome powers of nature. Scholars differed about the qualities of the forces that gave stability to the cosmos, with some theorizing about "mechanical" and other "vital" forces, and similar interpretations were extended to the human body in the same spirit of investigation.[2] The Hippocratic-Galenic medical system increasingly came under attack through inquiries into the nature of the body, the source of illness, and the methodology of healing.

The representation of the body as a machine challenged the conceptualizations of both Hippocrates and Galen and thus threatened long-held medical beliefs. Most mechanical understandings of the body built upon the labors of Andreas Vesalius (1514–1564). Vesalius occupied the chair of anatomy at the University of Padua, where he published *De fabrica humani corporis*, an anatomical masterpiece that identified numerous errors in Galen's understanding of human anatomy and became the classic text for several hundred years. William Harvey (1578–1657) further helped to undermine the Hippocratic-Galenic image of the body in his explanation of the circulation of blood. Dispensing with the idea of a flow of humors, Harvey envisioned the heart as a "pump," a representation of the body as machine. This mechanistic image required an understanding of the shape, size, and movements of its parts and, in particular, a study of anatomy.[3] Different scholars conceived of the primary "systems" that dominated the mechanical body, and systematists advanced mechanical or neuromuscular theories to demonstrate the general laws that governed its functions.[4] Anatomical and physiological investigations produced much of this knowledge. Albrecht von Haller, for example, envisioned the body's systems as dominated by irritable muscular and sensitive nervous fibers, an approach that stimulated the study of neurophysiology. William Cullen, following in this vein, focused on the nervous system, which he said needed balance and stimulation to promote good health. For these and other systematists, disease originated in the disorder of systems and was generalized throughout the body.

Other thinkers acknowledged the systems that operated in the body but believed that disease often sprang from disturbances caused by vital forces, or the "anima." In this framing, diseases were thought to be localized, as opposed to the more generalized diseases of the systemic perspective. Paracelsus (1493–1541) is often cited as an early and influential proponent of vital forces. His study of alchemy persuaded him that disease resulted when "an independent, self-willed spirit of a body organ . . . [becomes] incapacitated"; the physician would thus need to act as a "substitute alchemist" who administers "chemically prepared remedies" to correct the incapacitated organ.[5] The Germanic Pietist Georg Ernst Stahl (1660–1734), in rejecting the primacy of the mechanistic body, viewed the anima as a constantly active force, ordained by God to serve as a conscious protector of the body that directed mechanical activities to ensure organic unity. For Stahl, disease was a disturbance of the vital functions, provoked by maladies of the soul.[6] François-Joseph-Victor Broussais de Sauvages believed that God had imparted an inner, organizing principle to the body, which was too mechanistic to have an autonomous motion.[7]

Whereas systematists tended to have a more secular image of the body, Paracelsians and proponents of vital forces frequently brought Christianity into their medical analyses. Even Descartes, who is often considered a leading proponent of mechanistic understandings, can be seen to fit within this category insofar as he saw the body as a machine created by God and the human soul as different from the animal soul. And Isaac Newton, whose mechanistic images dominated the rethinking of the natural world, saw the "first cause" as nonmechanical.[8] As will be discussed later in this volume, some physicians in Latin America (most frequently of Conservative political affiliation) would draw upon the labor of these and other medical philosophers for understandings that would be compatible with their own religious beliefs. Those who tended toward liberalism would be more comfortable with mechanical images of the body's function. Perdomo clearly fit in the Conservative camp.

Because most of these European thinkers taught medicine in universities, they tended to be more scholarly and less practical in their approach to healing. By contrast, Thomas Sydenham (1624–1689) relied more upon observation and clinical study for his medical understanding—an approach that earned him the label of "the English Hippocrates." He believed that "the art of medicine was to be properly learnt only from its practice and its exercise," preferably at the patient's bedside.[9] Hermann Boerhaave, who built the University of Leiden into a premier center of medical education, found much to praise in Sydenham's emphasis on clinical observation. Having initially studied chemistry, he brought both the principles of that field and elements of Sydenham's theory into the university; Roy Porter suggests that Boerhaave "synthesized Sydenham for university use."[10] The University of Edinburgh took a similar approach to medical education.

By the early years of the nineteenth century, knowledge of anatomy and physiology and methods of clinical observation in hospitals came together in France to shape the clinic as the locus of medical investigation. Schools of medicine sought to join education obtained at the bedside of patients in hospitals with knowledge acquired in the class-room. The increased sophistication of anatomical studies in the clinic led to an emphasis on pathology, which represented disease as "*abnor-malities* in the *structure* and *function* of body organs and system."[11] Morbid anatomy, which revealed the effects of disease on the body, became linked with manifestations of the same disease in a living body in what has been called the "anatomoclinical method." Physicians, with their privileged knowledge, were taught to see the person less as sick and more as diseased or perhaps even objectified as the disease itself. Michel Foucault describes this as "the physician's gaze," refer-ring to a process by which knowledge changes how doctors see and speak.[12] This French approach to medicine would strongly influence the generation of scholars who shaped nineteenth-century scientific medical knowledge in Colombia, on which many critiques of Perdomo were based.

In the generation during which Perdomo traveled through Co-lombia and Ecuador, the craft of surgery underwent far-reaching changes. Eighteenth-century studies of chemicals and gases led to the development of new forms of anesthesia in the mid-nineteenth cen-tury, removing from surgery much of the terror that had accompa-nied it for so many years. The people who spoke of Perdomo's capacity to operate without causing pain alluded to this terror. Although anes-thesia had not been introduced into Colombia or Ecuador by the 1870s, physicians were certainly aware of experiments with ether and other gases. In time, they would learn of antisepsis, which is generally associated with Joseph Lister.

Equally profound changes occurred in the understandings of dis-ease in the second half of the nineteenth century. Louis Pasteur and Robert Koch (among others) developed germ theory and an under-standing of microbiology that led to radically new treatment method-ologies. Germ theory assisted in the rise of the laboratory as a counterpart to the clinic, preparing the way for a new emphasis upon pharmacology. These understandings, most of which emerged in the 1860s and beyond, served to further underpin the biological medi-cine of the twentieth century. The medical knowledge created by ra-tionalism would shape the minds of the physicians who criticized Perdomo and his adherence to a distinct medical ideology.

The Introduction of Enlightened
Medical Ideology in the Andes

The introduction of rationalism and scientific medical knowledge into the northern Andes fostered the slow creation of a new medical system. From its initial propagation in a limited number of institutions of higher education during the late colonial period, this medical ideology eventually made its presence felt in hospitals, clinics, and private practice. The new beliefs were not without their critics, but the favoritism shown to the novel (and European) intellectual current by leading Latin American officials greatly enhanced the institutionalization of scientific medicine. By the 1870s, therefore, the rationalist medical ideology was firmly entrenched in universities, medical journals, and professional associations of a corps of medical practitioners.[13] The Colombian government gave legal authority and support to this project by the end of the century, and Ecuadorean officials followed suit soon thereafter. The top-down institutionalization of a new medical ideology created significant differences between elite and popular medicine and helped to shape a new system of medical pluralism.

The transformation of medicine began later and developed more slowly in Latin America than in Europe. Imperial filters hindered the introduction of new beliefs until a fresh generation of physicians brought enlightened medical ideology into New Granadan medical schools in the last third of the eighteenth century. The premier member of that generation, José Celestino Mutis (1732–1808), arrived in New Granada in 1761 from Spain to serve as physician to Viceroy Pedro Messía de la Cerda. Within a year, he had assumed a chair in mathematics at the Colegio Major del Rosario (the Rosario), a position that he held off and on for four decades. Mutis also was a member of the 1783 botanical expedition sponsored by Charles III to survey natural resources, which symbolized the influx of Enlightenment ideas and programs into the Indies under the auspices of the Bourbon monarchs. During the expedition, Mutis helped to investigate and classify plants that might be of medicinal value. His notable accomplishment was the "discovery" of the *chinchona* tree in New Granada, a source of quinine for the treatment of malaria.[14] Over 150 years earlier, "Jesuit bark" had transformed the treatment of malaria in Europe, with significant financial and medical repercussions.

Like many Enlightenment physicians, Mutis generally preferred knowledge and scientific investigations over quotidian medical practices. He taught some courses on medicine at the Rosario, but his ideas apparently antagonized various officials. He declined an offer to serve as *protomedicato*, being more concerned with his scientific investigations and, according to some interpreters, less concerned with the practicalities of medicine. He did publish several pamphlets in the early 1780s, including a study on inoculations that earned the support of Viceroy Antonio Caballero y Gongora. Not all Bogotanos welcomed the new treatment methodology with open arms, however, leading Mutis to complain about certain officials who were disposed to criticize "anything that is new" despite its practical and proven applications.[15] He was largely correct in this assessment, as educators tended to view innovations with conservative skepticism.

In 1787, Viceroy Caballero y Gongora proposed the establishment of a university dedicated to medical training. Three years later, Sebastián López Rúiz informed Charles III of the backward state of medicine in New Granada and the ignorance of the area's physicians, excepting Mutis from the latter category.[16] Pedro Ibáñez, the most frequently cited authority on this time, observes that surgery during the colonial period was the exclusive domain of "barbers and some curanderos," most of whom belonged to the "mixed races." A few phlebotomists began to practice toward the end of the colonial period, but the most advanced surgeries consisted of cesareans that, by royal *cedula*, had to be performed according to a pamphlet from the early colonial period. He contends that "this most difficult area of human knowledge" was "monopolized by ignorant, barbarian indigenous healers."[17] Mutis had a somewhat more favorable view of the popular *curanderos*, suggesting that they delivered important components of health care to the general populace and that some Romance surgeons did a good job. In any case, he stated, they would have to do until specialists were trained.[18]

Padre Miguel de la Isla, director of the Hospital de San Juan de Dios, bridged the worlds of knowledge and practice that Mutis had trouble crossing. De la Isla, who had risen from the post of orderly at San Juan de Dios and who had been trained earlier at the Rosario, linked scientific investigations and health care delivery in a less radical manner than Mutis did.[19]

After years of stop-and-go reform efforts, significant changes in medical education were made as the Rosario opened a new program of medical studies in 1801.[20] Sponsored by Mutis and de la Isla, it was modeled after similar curricula adopted in Spain in 1795. This program stressed more pragmatic, hands-on medical experience and less scholastic inquiry. It also reflected Mutis's desire to improve surgical practices in the colonies. In an important move the medical education received at the Rosario was formally linked to clinical experience at the Hospital de San Juan de Dios, a relationship that would be enhanced over the course of the nineteenth century. The first-year curriculum of medical theory engaged theoretical anatomy in the college and its practical application in the hospital; medical institutions were studied in the second year; the third year focused on practical and general pathology, and Hippocratic doctrines were taught in the fourth and fifth years. Medical students would then undergo three years of practice at the hospital.[21] Romance surgeons, who studied in Spanish rather than Latin, covered anatomy in the first year, surgical institutions in the second, and surgical practice in the third.[22] The authors of this plan openly proclaimed the transition from traditional to new medical ideologies. Scholasticism, they said, was a dead weight on the medical profession: "In place of Latin authors and metaphysics, students should acquire knowledge of the exact sciences and of natural history, which are more important to a practical, rather than speculative, career."[23]

The texts used in the medical school suggest both the introduction of new concepts and the persistence of traditional understandings. Hippocrates continued to be taught but so, too, was Boerhaave, whose methods fused mechanical and humoral techniques. The system of medical education linked clinical experience, hospitals, and extended classroom study in a manner that reflected the innovations in university training developed at Boerhaave's University of Leiden. Students read the work of Friedrich Hoffman (1660–1742), who, like Boerhaave, espoused mechanistic understandings but whose

Pietism envisioned God as giving animus to an active body. Texts by the French skin specialist Jean Louis Alibert (1768–1837), Sydenham, Broussais de Sauvages, and Gabriel Andral were cited. Thus, though humoral medicine continued to shape professional instruction, rationalist interpretations had been placed at the core of the newly invigorated Colombian educational system.[24]

The medical program at the Rosario graduated its first students in 1805. By the end of the decade, it had produced the first generation of Colombian physicians, including Juan María Pardo, Francisco Quijano, Benito Osorio, and José Félix Merizalde. As director of the program, Padre de la Isla viewed the acceptance of this formal training and the willingness of Bogotano youths to enroll in the university as signs of a greater acceptance of the virtues of the medical trade by the colonial elite.[25] After de la Isla's death in 1807, Gil de Tejada, an early graduate of the program, assumed many of the padre's responsibilities. A large number of students at the Rosario had not yet finished their training when the war for independence disrupted the capital. Merizalde endowed a chair at San Bartolomé with his own funds after 1812, but the Rosario remained open only sporadically until the end of the war. Students served in both patriot and royalist armies, though more often with the former than the latter.

Polemics and Problems in the Early National Period

Foreign physicians helped to accelerate the transformation of Bogotá's system of medical education after Independence, but their preferred treatment methodologies also generated ideological disputes in the medical community. For example, Pierre Paul Broc and Bernardo Daste began teaching medical sciences in 1823 under a government contract. These men helped to implant the influence of French medicine in Colombian educational institutions, especially in their adherence to the methods of Broussais, one of the last great systematists. Broussais envisioned most illnesses as the outward manifestation of digestive irritations. He recommended radical intervention, most frequently voluminous bloodletting.[26] Broc taught anatomy at the Hospital de San Juan de Dios; Daste taught surgery at the same location; and the

Scot Ninian Richard Cheyne, who had arrived with the British Legion, taught surgery in the schools. Cheyne defended his fellow countryman John Brown in a series of bitter polemics over proper medical ideologies. Brown, also a systematist, viewed the organs of the body as being in a constant state of excitement or irritation. Believing that illness was an increase or decrease of the normally excited body, he contended that large doses of alcohol, opium, or other potent drugs would help to return it to its normal state. Cheyne defended Brown's theories with vigor, but the French influence dominated the government-sponsored faculty of medicine at the Universidad Central de Bogotá, established in 1827; its primary text was a translation from the French.[27] Similar French influences prevailed in other urban medical practices. Significantly, the responsibility vested in the *protomedicato* was transferred to the new school of medicine, an important step in the shifting relationship between state authority and the medical community.[28]

The differing medical beliefs of the French and British physicians promptly embroiled their Colombian counterparts in public discord. In 1824, Merizalde, an ardent and skilled polemicist, took offense at a statement in the *Gaceta de Colombia* that Bogotá lacked trained physicians. Presuming that the charge originated with Broc, Merizalde alleged that the government was not getting its money's worth from the French physicians. Broc, he claimed, taught anatomy straight from the work of Alexis Boyer, with no insight of his own. Moreover, he charged that Broc's physiological theories came verbatim from an old dictionary and that the Frenchman seemed to be unaware of a new edition. He also stated that Broc failed to give exams and allowed students who had not yet learned medicine to practice on the poor at the Hospital de Caridad.[29]

Broc did not defend himself, but Daste came to his compatriot's aid. The French surgeon insisted that although students assisted at the hospital, they were allowed to practice medicine only within certain limits. As for Broc's teaching abilities, Daste stated that Merizalde was simply wrong.[30] For his part, Merizalde acknowledged that Daste was a titled physician and that he should know his profession, but he accused the Frenchman of using a poor surgical methodology that led to unnecessary deaths. In addition, he said that Daste lacked the honor to admit his error in allowing students to practice surgery.[31]

Professors at the Universidad Central trained a second generation of scientific physicians, several of whom would play active roles in the institutionalization of Colombian medicine—and in the disputes surrounding Perdomo. Many members of this generation traveled to France to further their education, bringing back to Colombia French anatomoclinical practices. This method joined the construction of case histories—through observation, investigation, and laboratory inquiries—with pathological anatomy, or the search for lesions or disorders on organs that would reveal a particular disease. For the clinicians, disease was not external to the patient but in the body. Through the case study the infirm person was constructed as a patient with a medical problem—a problem identifiable to Foucault's physician's gaze. With intensive training and clinical experience, the physician could develop the ability to perceive diseased bodies and effect their cure.[32] Byron Good, expanding on Foucault's concept, notes that "learning medicine is developing knowledge of the distinctive life world and requires an entry into a distinctive reality system." Medical education "changes the brains" of medical students, "forcing them to acquire new ways of seeing, speaking, and writing." Criticizing Foucault, he argues that medical knowledge is not just perception but a "medium of experience, a mode of engagement with the world."[33] Once an individual is educated with this new knowledge, other ways of knowing seem less tenable; in its extreme, he contends, knowledge creates a truth system with no intellectual flexibility or tolerance.

The faculty of the school of medicine displayed an arrogance toward nonscientific medical knowledge that had not been apparent in Mutis or de la Isla. In 1830, for example, Juan María Pardo revealed his scientific superiority in a public lecture: "The study of medicine was absolutely unknown in this capital until 1802; one could not find a single [doctor] whose services were guided by [medical] principles; dangerous prescriptions were taken from ancient, rancid texts, complicated brews contrary to the art of curation were administered by charlatans who supposedly could know and determine the situation of their patients with a simple view of their urine; these men drove thousands of victims to their graves."[34] A few years earlier, Merizalde had criticized colonial instructors for teaching the principles of the "terrible" chemical Galenic medicine, modified only in respect to a different climate. For Pardo, medicine had progressed so much that the metaphysical teachings of the prima and vísperas chairs now seemed absurd. Modern students needed to know pathology and chemistry.[35]

Antonio Vargas Reyes

No one personifies the lifeways and attitudes of this second generation of scientific physicians better than Antonio Vargas Reyes. Born in 1816 to a well-to-do loyalist family, Vargas Reyes attended both the Colegio de Nuestra Señora del Rosario and the Colegio de San Bartolomé before settling upon a medical career. After beginning medical school at the Rosario in 1834, he so impressed his professors that he was teaching anatomy within two years. Although titled as a doctor in 1837, he did not receive authorization to practice medicine until 1841, by which point he had accumulated extensive surgical experience, especially while serving in the Liberal army during the 1839–1841 civil war. Vargas Reyes left for Paris in 1842, where he undertook four years of extensive training in the anatomoclinical method. By the time that he returned to Colombia in 1847, his reputation in diagnostics and surgery was widespread. He assumed the position of physician at the Hospital de Caridad and professor of special pathology at the Rosario. Vargas Reyes promptly set about remaking the hospital in the French tradition.[36]

Despite its heady beginnings, the Universidad Central never reached its desired status as the seat of Colombian medical education, nor were the careers of Vargas Reyes and his colleagues free of trouble. A new generation of liberal politicians stood in the way of the modest success of this medical enterprise. The most fervent liberals wished to remove state and institutional control from many areas of social life. The Church was therefore seen as a particularly worthy opponent, especially in systems of education. A leading Liberal daily alleged that the educational system was so corrupted by Catholic teachings that complete freedom of education was the only hope for the country.[37] And by what right, the liberals argued, did the state require an educational degree to practice law or medicine? None, according to the Congress of 1850, which lifted all restrictions on the teaching of arts, letters, and sciences. The Law of May 15, 1850, which removed the need for a license to practice any profession except pharmacy, threw medical education into chaos.

Physicians who had led the efforts to formalize medical education suffered a fundamental setback with this legislation. The state had played a central role in formal medicine during the colonial era and had signaled its willingness to do so in the national period, at least until the onset of liberal reforms. This led Vargas Reyes, Nicolas A. Vega, and others to found *La Lanceta*, seeking a "union of physicians" "that would protect their reciprocal interests, and also that of science, both of which are in the [best] interests of humanity."[38] (The paper took its name from the similarly named London publication.) The editors outlined several goals for *La Lanceta*: to serve as a forum for medical progress, to combat charlatanism, to increase the status of the medical profession, to promote sound systems of medical education, and to stimulate young men to continue their medical studies. This last point directly addressed the Law of May 15, 1850, because the professors at the Universidad Central had encountered severe difficulties in recruiting students who would practice medicine without any title or training. The editors feared that the lack of a medical organization would "entice [the youth] on the road to charlatanism and false knowledge."[39] Within one month of its founding and the listing of medical courses available at the school of medicine, the paper reported that three classes were canceled due to a lack of students.[40]

For this group of physicians, the well-being of the medical profession was closely linked with the perceived dangers of charlatanism. Because the achievements of professional doctors were poorly known, the editors of *La Lanceta* insisted that empirics and charlatans were growing in popularity. Merizalde had earlier defined a charlatan as "an empiric who presents himself as a titled medical doctor."[41] For Vargas Reyes and the other editors, a charlatan was one who sought "the mysterious" instead of the "true knowledge" of science.[42] (This language would be paralleled by Rivas in his critique of Perdomo a generation later.) The editors further stated that possessing empirical knowledge that originated in practice did not warrant the status of a doctor. For a surgeon, "it is not just the mechanical part of the operation that must be attended to; it is necessary to know the science, to compare, to induce, and to reason . . . [because] for a practical physician, *the body is transparent.*"[43]

It is difficult to imagine a more cogent sense of the medical gaze than that expressed in this last phrase—"the body is transparent." The physician's gaze revealed the rational function (or dysfunction) of the body, enabling a cure to be determined. In this phrase and in the articles published in *La Lanceta*, the infusion of European medical ideology is evident. Indeed, the six issues of the paper were filled with articles on "medical progress." The work of M. Champouillon on tuberculosis offered promise for the treatment of pulmonary afflictions; a reprint from the *Bulletin de Thérapeutique* told of the use of ipecac to treat dysentery; a series of articles praised the use of chloroform in deliveries and surgery, downplaying the number of fatalities associated with the gas, and Galvanism was the subject of a piece from London. The numerous medical reports typically included a case study, a description of the treatment methodology, and the recipe for appropriate treatment doses. Most of the reports originated in France or England, but some came from the United States, and a few Colombian physicians reported their findings as well. If these articles are indicative, prominent physicians were fully conversant with the emerging scientific medical ideology.[44]

Because the Law of 1850 threatened the progress inherent in that discourse, the editors of *La Lanceta* lobbied (in vain) for the repeal of the law. As the fortunes of medical education declined, Merizalde, Vargas Reyes, and Andrés María Pardo tried to start a school of medicine that would combine the facilities of the Rosario and San Bartolomé, but they had only limited success.

The Law of 1850 certainly alienated many doctors, but it was a relatively minor item on the Liberal agenda. The Era of Liberal Reform had begun in 1846 when Conservative president Tomás Cipriano de Mosquera introduced a series of economic reforms, including a plan to drastically lower tariff rates. When it came to power in 1849, the Liberal party sponsored a wave of reforms that did away with most vestiges of the colonial order. Liberal economic principles provided the rationale for the elimination of monopolies on tobacco and *aguardiente*, the decentralization of certain economic rents, the abolition of the *resguardo* (corporate landholding), and the elimination of the *alcabala* (sales tax). In the area of government, suffrage was extended to all males over twenty-one, the direct election of departmental governors was mandated, and the initial steps toward federalism were taken. The legislature proclaimed the abolition of slavery and freedom of the press and of speech. The most contentious reforms dealt with the Church, which was officially separated from the state in keeping with the concept of religious freedom. In 1850 the Jesuits were ordered to leave Colombia. The purely federalist constitution of 1858 helped provoke the 1859–1862 civil war, whereupon further reforms removed Church rents, closed monasteries and convents, and limited the secular authority of clerics.[45] By 1865 liberal reforms had transformed the formal structure and social principles of the country, paving the way for the "Radical Olympus," the period of Radical liberal rule that lasted until 1886.

Turbulent economic and political conditions frustrated the efforts to institutionalize scientific medicine. In particular, the civil war of the late 1850s hampered the physicians' efforts to establish a new school of medicine and to gain public recognition for their trade. In June 1864, however, these men began publishing the *Gaceta Médica de Bogotá*. Six months later, in February 1865, they opened the Escuela de Medicina, a private institution with linkages to the Hospital de Caridad. Twenty students enrolled initially, with fifteen in the course on anatomy. Bogotá's medical elite, many of whom either had dominated or would dominate the profession, taught in the school.[46] They offered a wide selection of courses, many requiring clinical practice at the Hospital de Caridad. By 1866, Abraham Aparicio had graduated from the program, followed shortly thereafter by several others.[47] Despite the school's success, however, complaints that its high cost blocked worthy aspirants to medical school soon surfaced.

The linkages between the paper and the school became more apparent in June 1865 when the paper's name was changed to the *Gaceta Médica*, "the mouthpiece of the Escuela de Medicina." The editors had the same goals as for the paper's 1852 predecessor, including disseminating medical progress, building rapport within the medical corps, and lobbying the government to recognize the medical profession and block empiricism and charlatanism. To this end, Vargas Reyes reported that he was learning minor surgery (bleeding and tooth removal) so that he could "take this part of medicine away from the domain of the charlatans, those who have always practiced in an absurd, routine, and homicidal manner."[48] More Colombians were published in the *Gaceta Médica* than in *La Lanceta*, although French contributions still predominated, much as might be expected with Vargas Reyes as its chief editor. He noted that "without pathological anatomy, without the opening of cadavers, it is impossible to be a physician; everything would be subject to capriciousness and routine. The human body is a great book which we can study and [thus] learn helpful lessons."[49] Although the paper folded in 1867, it had initiated a nearly continuous appearance of medical publications in Bogotá.[50]

At the apparent high point of liberalism, the Colombian legislature began to retreat and adopt a more pragmatic course of action. It yielded to pressures from physicians to approve the establishment of a faculty of medicine at the Universidad Nacional in Bogotá in September 1867. Six colleges, four of which were already in operation, constituted the university. The Escuela de Medicina was transformed almost entirely into the university's medical school, under the direction of Vargas Reyes, with full facilities for formal medical training at the San Juan de Dios hospital. It opened in early 1868.[51] Once gained, the school's authority to foster a particular pattern of knowledge would be ardently defended.

Homeopathy

Just as the advocates of rational medicine succeeded in gaining state support for their educational endeavors, a distinct scientific medical ideology known as homeopathy made its presence known in the Colombian capital. Samuel Hahnemann (1755–1843), a German physician, pronounced the tenets of homeopathic medicine in the 1790s.

Hahnemann claimed that illness originated in disturbances of the "vital force" and manifested itself in symptoms or phenomena that a homeopathic physician would seek to alleviate by applying the law of *similia similibus curantur* (like is cured by like). Symptoms would be treated by small doses of botanical or chemical prescriptions to produce symptoms like those of the presenting illness. For example, a mild fever might be treated by a dose of quinine, which produced such a fever and was thought to cure it. Similarly, sulfur was used both to produce and to cure skin rashes. According to homeopaths, such medicines allowed the vital force to restore health. Hahnemann ardently opposed most medical systems of the day for their inability to improve the art of healing and for the violence of their treatments. His ideas and those of his followers were also subjected to considerable criticism from physicians of the emerging scientific method.[52]

José Peregrino Sanmiguel, the father of Colombian homeopathy, learned of this medical ideology in the 1830s. In 1840 he traveled to Ecuador, where he worked as a homeopathic physician in the army of Juan José Flores. He returned to Colombia in 1845, where others had been converted to this system of medical beliefs. In contrast to biomedical practitioners, homeopathic doctors praised the Law of 1850 because liberty of industry gave them the freedom to practice. Although Sanmiguel faced considerable opposition from biomedical believers, he, Salvador Alvarez, Saturnino de Castillo, Marcelino Liévano, and Ignacio Pereira established the Instituto de Homeopatía to train other physicians by 1865. At that time, five homeopathic pharmacies existed in Bogotá, most likely run by the five physicians who started the institute.[53] Numerous homeopathic physicians would later defend Perdomo, perhaps because of their shared sense of the anima or because they faced comparable political obstacles from allopathic doctors.

Despite having high-profile political support, homeopaths insisted that an alliance among scientific medical physicians (whom they labeled allopaths), university professors, and the state was blocking their "natural" development. The charge appears to be accurate. The Cundinamarcan legislature's Law of August 15, 1869, which created the Junta Central de Beneficiencia to regulate all state charity institutions, denied the Instituto de Homeopatía the right to use a wing of the Hospital de Caridad.[54] In 1874, Marcelino Liévano organized a petition to the legislature, requesting permission to establish a homeopathic clinic in the hospital. Biomedical physicians at the university helped to defeat the proposal as they aggressively sought to impede the expansion of homeopathic practices.

Ecuador

The introduction of enlightened medical ideologies into Ecuador followed a pattern similar to that in New Granada, a testament to the colonial information filter. Charles III revoked the authority of both the Universidad de San Fulgencio and the Universidad de San Gregorio Magno to teach medicine, leaving only the Dominican-sponsored Universidad de Santo Tomás the right to offer medical instruction.[55] Its curriculum began to change in the 1780s when the works of Boerhaave were introduced, albeit using the scholastic method. A new plan of studies departed from those traditional methods in 1791, but the curricular reform was stalled by the death of the school's dean. *Protomedicato* Bernardo Delgado assumed the responsibilities and continued the education reform in the years before Independence.[56] Despite these initiatives, however, few physicians were graduated. The most notable alumnus, Francisco Javier Eugenio de Santa Cruz y Espejo (1747–1796), claimed that no "true" chairs of medicine existed in the country.[57]

Espejo quickly became Ecuador's most enlightened medical thinker, fomenting the same intellectual turmoil as did Mutis, although on a smaller scale. His writings were replete with references to Boerhaave and other European scholars, suggesting his receptivity to new ways of thought.[58] Espejo lived in Bogotá for three years (1788–1791), where he undoubtedly collaborated with the New Granadan savant.[59] On one occasion the *cabildo*, acting on a request from some physicians and Bethlemites, asked that Espejo edit the works of Francisco Gil, viceroy of Peru. The same body rejected the finished product, which reflected Espejo's condemnation of Gil's more traditional medical ideology.[60]

The transformation of official medicine begun in the late colonial period continued into the early national period. Institutional practices, particularly those associated with hospitals, were given a boost by the war. The contributions of military hospitals revitalized both civilian and war-related institutions of healing. Private practices supplemented more public services for a limited segment of the population. The *cabildo* continued to exert a powerful medical influence in Quito, in contrast to Bogotá where a fledgling medical institution was supported by a first generation of professional physicians.[61]

Changes in medical instruction were less immediate. Juan Manuel de la Gala opened a faculty of medicine at the Universidad Central in 1827, officially taking on some of the charges of the *protomedicato*. By 1830 the faculty had won the right to license physicians and inspect *boticas*, and their decisions were enforced by the municipal police, who came under the *cabildo*'s jurisdiction.[62] Pharmacists were exempted from having to take classes because too few were available. They did, however, have to pass an examination to be licensed.[63] The faculty members at the Universidad Central proved to be an important force in the emerging scientific medical community, but their influence declined precipitously by the 1840s. At least one reason for the decline lay in the ongoing antagonism to medical ideology. The faculty strove to convince the populace of the efficacy of science and its superiority over empiricism. In this project, professional physicians struggled against two traditions—the powerful presence of the Church and the equally important empiric tradition. Clerics throughout the country believed that healing was part of their ministry, and they were loath to relinquish their medical influence. As Gualberto Arcos notes, physicians "had to constantly fight against the heterogeneous mass of [unlicensed] doctors, surgeons, healers, herbalists, and bleeders that had invaded the Republic . . . many of them, without fear or scruples, and with only a little scientific knowledge, prescribed drugs and assisted the ill."[64]

As the university lost its short-lived influence on the direction of medical authority, the municipal council reemerged as a potent force. Physicians now served as members of the council, so its deliberations reflected the influences of the same people who shaped the university.

The council continued to name *médicos de pobres* (physicians of the poor), including, at the time of Perdomo's visit, Manuel Regalado, Manuel María Bueno, and Carlos Mera. The *cabildo* also regulated and examined the city's hospitals,[65] an effort that was handicapped by a shortage of funds. The council used licensing fees to support itself, often boosting those fees to meet budget expenses. These increases sometimes met with opposition; in 1867, for instance, merchants joined wood carriers to protest a recent tax increase.[66]

Fundamental changes in medical instruction did not take place until the 1870s, when two French instructors were invited by President Gabriel García Moreno to reorganize the medical school. Etienne Gayraud and Domingo Domec moved away from theoretical medicine and put more emphasis on laboratories and clinics. Both taught surgery according to European methods, including the use of chloroform, antiseptics, and Listerine. Their program of studies, established in 1874, marked the beginning of the era of modern scientific medicine in Ecuador.[67] It included courses on experimental physiology, pathology, and microbiology and focused considerable attention on clinical experience.[68]

The Institutionalization of Scientific Medicine

Despite the fact that most Colombians and Ecuadoreans neither knew of nor agreed with the tenets of scientific medicine, that medical ideology began to be institutionalized over the last third of the nineteenth century. This was by no means a continuous, uninterrupted process but was instead fitful and not concluded until well into the twentieth century. The authority of knowledge vested in institutions of higher education, the transformation of the medical corps, and the authorization of scientific medicine with the legal power of the state all represented critical facets of the process of institutionalization. Although each facet developed along a different trajectory in the two countries, the process was similar in both, especially as it represented state support for rationalist beliefs.[69]

The granting of official support for new schools of medicine marked a critical step in the institutionalization of scientific medicine. This step took place in Colombia in the late 1860s and in Ecuador several years later. The curriculum of the school of medicine at the Universidad Nacional in Bogotá forced students, in Byron Good's words, into a distinct reality system. In contrast to the curriculum of the private school of medicine, the course schedule presumed a better background in science for its students.[70] First-year students took three courses: general anatomy and histology, a first course in special anatomy, and physiology. Second-year courses included three on pathology, one on anatomy, and a section of one on minor surgery. Courses on *materia medica* and therapeutics, external pathology, and topographic anatomy and operative medicine filled the third year. Several of the courses after the first year were augmented by clinics at the Hospital de Caridad. Fourth-year courses on obstetrics and special pathologies for women and children, public and private hygiene, and forensic medicine completed the curriculum. Students had only to pass oral and practical exams to earn their Doctor of Medicine and Surgery degree.[71] Practically the same curriculum was installed in the school of medicine in Quito several years later. In both Ecuador and Colombia, state support for instruction in scientific medicine was firmly entrenched by the 1870s.

The Universidad Nacional served as a fundamental force in the institutionalization of science in Colombia. It matriculated 1,623 people in law, engineering, the natural sciences, and medicine during the 1870s. The school of medicine graduated more than any other division (more than one-third of the total),[72] and many of its alumni promptly joined a professional society.

As it had during the previous thirty years, the French anatomo-clinical ideology dominated medical instruction. The curriculum required linkages with hospitals, reinforcing a relationship that had been forged in 1802. Church-sponsored hospitals, notably the Hospital de San Juan de Dios, served as the primary colonial institutions of medical charity and became the nineteenth-century clinics. Although San Juan de Dios had experienced considerable institutional unrest in the generations after 1750, its continued existence enabled reformers to slowly change its mission. Viceroy Pedro Mendinueta separated San Juan de Dios's military hospital from its Hospital de Caridad in 1797. Several years later the 1802 plan put the Hospital de Caridad at the disposal of the professors of the school of medicine at the Rosario. Not only would their students make clinical use of the patients at the hospital, but they would also use the cadavers of the deceased in their anatomy classes.[73]

The Hospital de Caridad, in spite of its association with the school of medicine, continued its charitable religious functions. Two appointed physicians attended to diagnoses, prescriptions, and surgery, assisted by nurses who were generally religious practitioners. The nurses, in turn, were assisted by various *religiosas* (lay practitioners) who were the "natural servants of the poor." Four lay practitioners were responsible for bleeding, plasters, and prescriptions.[74] Three clinics were supervised by the faculty members, who had authority over the nurses in the clinics during the day, when scientific medicine dominated treatment. At night, however, Catholic healing ideologies were more influential as the nurses reasserted their control. Significantly, any unclaimed cadavers would be available to the professors of anatomy for their courses.[75] By 1887 four clinics associated with the school of medicine operated within the Hospital de Caridad: general pathology and minor surgery, internal and external pathology, special surgery, and obstetrics and juvenile medicine.[76]

Charitable institutions underwent significant changes in their missions in the late eighteenth century, initiating the process through which Christian charity came to be supplemented by "public health." Whereas Christian charity had been conceived of as both a private act representing a gift to Christ and a public mission of the Church, the "enlightened charity" of the late eighteenth century represented a response to civil problems that would, in time, become programs of health under state control. The colonial *hospicio* (hospice), for example, had been designed to instill habits of industry among the poor, thereby improving social tranquility.[77] Two workshops, one for males and the other for females, were established in the 1770s, with a foundling house transferred to the women's wing. These *hospicios* failed to survive the institutional crisis of the Independence period, although the Casa de Refugio, with overt intentions of offering industrial education to the poor, opened in 1833. By the 1850s over two-thirds of the 200 to 250 charges in the workshop were foundlings,[78] suggesting both the failure of its institutional mission and the slow replacement of the Church's charitable presence by state authorities.

The Cundinamarcan state legislature authorized the creation of the Junta Central de Beneficencia to oversee all public charity institutions in 1869. These included the Hospital de Caridad, three leprosy asylums, the Casa de Refugio, and an asylum for indigents (male). The latter, housed in the Convento de San Diego, was placed until the control of Archbishop Vicente Arbeláez.[79] Three years later an asylum for female indigents was founded. In the early years, an average of 300 people passed through the two asylums. Each year in the 1870s almost 1,000 people entered the Hospital de Caridad, where the death rate was just over 15 percent.[80]

The clinics of the Hospital de Caridad were central to the anatomo-clinical method of the founders of the school of medicine, but that approach came under increasing scrutiny as the century progressed. Bacteriology, physiology, and histology—medical innovations that sustained germ theory—demanded more emphasis on laboratory analysis. Roberto Franco, who had studied at the Pasteur Institute, and Pablo García Medina, a devotee of Claude Bernard, helped to supplant the anatomoclinical method in the last decades of the nineteenth century. By the early 1900s, the laboratory had replaced the clinic as the focus of medical education.[81]

Associations paralleled the university as a means of separating social and professional medicine. Physicians at the Universidad Nacional helped to found the Sociedad de Medicina y Ciencias Naturales in the Colombian capital in 1873. The society had as its goals "the stimulation and promotion of the study of the medical and natural sciences in the country, to give body and unity to national scientific works, to offer solidarity to the medical community, and to promote respect for the mission of healing human illnesses."[82] Although the society declared its intention to remain conversant with international science, it also wished to promote a national science dedicated to particularly Colombian geographic and physical realities. Abraham Aparicio was selected as secretary, while Pío Rengifo edited the society's *Revista Médica*. The society sought to introduce new ideas into the country and help to spread them through its journal and by bringing physicians and scientists into its learned community. It declared a preference, however, for original works by national authors. In the late 1870s, Aparicio conducted a survey of doctors throughout the country, asking them about certain medical procedures and the status of medicine in their regions.[83] The promotion of a system of national medicine required, as the society's members saw it, a complete technical and ideological integration of domestic physicians into the practices of scientific medicine. As their predecessors had for years, many Colombian physicians of this period went abroad for much of their medical education, more often than not training in France. Indeed, French medical thought profoundly influenced this generation of physicians, especially in terms of the civilizing agency of science and the active role of a centralized medical authority under state auspices.[84] The *Revista Médica* carried translated articles from French, English, and U.S. journals. And many of the society's members became corresponding members of similar organizations in foreign countries.[85]

The Sociedad de Medicina y Ciencias Naturales proved to be an able promoter of scientific medicine. At the regional level, the Academia de Medicina of Medellín served a similar purpose, though the Bogotá organization was more influential at the national level. The academy operated on its own funds from 1873 until 1891, but in the latter year, it became the Academia Nacional de Medicina, and linkages to the government were formalized.[86] José María Buendia served as its first president, although he was soon replaced by García Medina.[87] In 1893 the academy sponsored the first National Congress of Medicine.[88]

The professionalization of medicine included efforts to limit those who could legally practice medicine. In Spain, for example, the faculty in several medical schools joined legal authorities in curbing the practice of nonscientific medicine. These authorities grouped a wide variety of healers into a prohibited category, defined only by a failure to operate with the ideology and structure of official medicine.[89] Vargas Reyes and other writers for *La Lanceta* had urged similar policies, then joined the campaign against homeopathy in the early 1870s. Healers such as Perdomo came under attack by professional physicians in both Colombia and Ecuador. However, not until the 1880s did the Regeneration government reverse earlier liberal policies and initiate the establishment of scientific medicine as Colombia's official medicine. When the constitution of 1886 was approved, the Law of 1850 was revoked, and a code requiring "proof of competency for the practice of medical or related professions" was enacted.[90] Science acquired the power of the state to enforce its "truths."[91] The next year, rules for the establishment of regulatory bodies were approved by the Congress, whereby legal oversight of educational requirements for licensing were established. The Regeneration regime also founded the Junta Central de Higiene to regulate public health, especially against the threat of epidemic disease.[92]

Twentieth-century governments continued to authorize scientific medicine. A 1905 executive decree established the formal regulation of doctors and surgeons, requiring that all physicians be titled by national faculties or their foreign equivalents. Despite pressures from biomedical physicians, homeopathic doctors were allowed to practice but only when titled by the Instituto de Homeopatía. The decree recognized that many areas of the country lacked titled physicians, and thus it gave nontitled ones the right to practice, providing that they supplied letters from academic doctors confirming their abilities; midwives were required to provide two letters of support. Violations of these regulations could earn a fine.[93] Law 83 of 1914 reinforced this decree, and Law 39 of 1920 created a title board to monitor the authorization of physicians.[94] Similar laws led to the licensing of nursing and midwifery.[95]

The "Revolution on the March" of President Alfonso López Pumarejo (1934–1938) reinforced this corpus of legislation, albeit with significant modifications. Law 67 of 1935 declared that the practice of medicine was a social function; doctors were therefore held civilly and legally responsible for the proper conduct of their profession. A central licensing board was set up to oversee similar departmental bodies, which would approve the titles of graduated doctors, surgeons, pharmacists, midwives, nurses, and dentists. Once again, despite the opposition of biomedical doctors, homeopathic medicine (with proper accreditation) was authorized. Violators of these regulations could now draw prison sentences in addition to fines. Law 67 also attempted to regulate "nonofficial" practices. Practitioners of the occult were required to both pass an examination by academic physicians and obtain permission from the Department of Hygiene. Interpreters of dreams, diviners, and fortune-tellers were banned outright.[96]

Although the state had sanctioned scientific medicine as official, it had a limited capacity to prevent nonofficial practices. Women giving birth, for example, might be assisted by midwives who "had the manual ability to receive babies" but lacked technical or antiseptic knowledge.[97] Further, although scientific doctors had gained legal authorization and public prestige, "the number of medical professionals remained too small to dent the impact of popular practitioners who remained vital to the welfare of the urban and rural poor of all ethnic groups."[98] Rural areas were barely affected by scientific medicine, which largely reached only the elite and members of the urban middle class.[99] Fortune-tellers and others operated without interruption.

The authorization and professionalization of scientific medicine followed a similar course in Ecuador. The Municipal Council of Quito, which had maintained many of its colonial privileges, continued to assert its control over issues of public health through the nineteenth century. This authority included the regulation of *boticas* and the licensing of physicians. The police commissioner, in the company of a professor from the medical faculty, inspected all *boticas*. This linkage of public interests and private medical concerns would be evident during Perdomo's visit, as physicians on the council sought to protect their profession from *curanderos* as well as from other physicians who sought the right to practice in Ecuador. Participants in an extensive debate acknowledged the right of Colombian physicians to work in the country—but only if they paid the appropriate fees and earned a license to do so. To ensure that foreigners would comply with these guidelines, the council regularly surveyed the city's medical community.[100] The 1885 police regulations on public health stipulated that "no one can practice medicine, surgery, pharmacy, phlebotomy, or obstetrics without the qualifications demanded by law, under the penalty of a fine of six to ten pesos, or three to seven days in prison, or a combination thereof."[101]

At the national level, Ecuador lagged behind Colombia in the professionalization of the medical community. The Medical Circle, recognized as a juridical entity in 1928, "was born to public life as a natural consequence of the era, a logical product of the medium that finds its definitive shape, not in cheap ideologies, but in the tangible reality of constituting a professional entity that was erected and sustained by the medical class."[102] Like the similar group in Colombia, the Medical Circle was founded to counter the illegal practice of the profession, to recruit young physicians into a unified body, to oppose medical and pharmaceutical charlatanism, and to work for a legislative system to regulate medicine. The Circle's journal argued that empirics were intolerable urban guests and habitual rural pests and that stricter laws on the illegal practice of medicine were needed. It also contended that pharmacies should be separated from medicine and that the practice of publishing prescriptions in the press should be stopped. Further, the Circle insisted upon the need for laws to stop midwives from using professional equipment, except those needed for injections.

Attitudes toward medicine revealed the broader transition being directed by Latin American intellectuals toward a reliance on natural science and away from the more traditional subservience to religious faith. This slow process took at least four generations to gain potency. The development of scientific medicine involved the creation of a body of practitioners trained in a new knowledge system, the construction of a medical infrastructure (schools, hospitals, clinics, and the like), the propagation of new ideologies through periodicals, and the linkage of scientific advocates by conferences and professional journals. Scientific medicine was professionalized over the course of the second half of the nineteenth century. Of equal significance was the authorization of this new medical ideology by the Colombian and Ecuadorean states. Liberal notions of professional activity were sharply curtailed so that a single medical ideology could be sanctioned by the state. These new belief systems were made official and were imbedded within legal structures that had the authority to penalize "deviants."

This process began to usurp the authority and social powers that healers within the colonial medical spectrum had enjoyed. Normally the pace of change reduced the possibility of social and other conflicts between the different medical systems. The visit of Perdomo to Bogotá, however, brought the ideological struggle into full public view.

3

The Life and Times of Miguel Perdomo Neira

The news [of Perdomo's arrival] immediately spread through the surrounding communities, and the following morning a multitude of curious and ill people were seen on all the roads that lead to the town; some came in improvised ambulances and others on miserable horses, and still others in decent carriages or on lively steeds. . . . The resulting scene inspired great curiosity in the spectator. The center of the plaza, the surrounding streets, and the patio and rooms of the house occupied by Perdomo were all filled with people. The agitation and movement of so many people; the pack mules tied together wherever possible; the ladies who showed off their fine clothes; the peasants dressed in their Sunday best; the men on horseback; and the beggars and all types of cripples; all this . . . formed a singularly spectacular display that brings to mind the happy mood of five or six Masses. In the midst of all this, Perdomo is busily occupied in visiting the sick who cannot come to him, or in listening to consultations, distributing medicine, and performing operations, using almost all of the free hours of the day to treat three or four hundred people.[1]

The public upheaval that accompanied Perdomo's arrival in Serrezuela, Colombia, upset the norms of this small town's social life. Nineteenth-century towns enjoyed a generally fixed festive calendar, marked by Masses, market days, saints' birthdays, *semana santa* (Holy Week), and, occasionally, voting. Visitors who caused significant departures from the usual routine were infrequent and often viewed with suspicion, and Perdomo, whose spectacularly public character commanded the attention of the entire town, clearly disrupted the

61

patterns of social life. Observers throughout Colombia and Ecuador recorded that the healer was received similarly elsewhere; when he visited Medellín, for example, a reporter noted that in the "streets and in the plazas, in the shops and in the kitchens, one hears only conversations about the appearance of this popular physician."[2] Scores and sometimes hundreds of people would flock to Perdomo's office to be cured of illness or injury. Of course, not everyone welcomed the healer so eagerly. Public authorities often expressed alarm at his arrival, usually putting police on alert. Political commentators frequently used a visit by Perdomo as an opportunity to laud (or critique) the issues of the day. And, in many towns, professional physicians sought to stop him from practicing medicine. The many and diverse reactions to Perdomo raise several questions. What caused the people of Serrezuela and other towns to seek assistance from this traveling healer? What had they heard that inspired such hope? What accounts for Perdomo's phenomenal popularity? Why did he provoke such heated opposition among public officials and professional doctors?

On one level the answers to these questions are simple. Some people believed that Perdomo could cure them of illnesses that no one else had been able to treat. Others counted upon his surgical skills, deemed by many to be miraculous. Still others knew that his drugs were powerful and effective. Moreover, everyone had heard that Perdomo did not charge for his services and that he insisted that it was his Christian obligation to heal for free. No wonder thousands of people longed for the arrival of the "people's doctor." But on another level, answers to these questions are very complex. They define the central themes of this analysis.

It is certainly true that few people were described as vividly as Perdomo was in his own time. Most people, of course, are almost invisible in the historical record: the vast majority of lives are only briefly referenced in baptismal, census, marriage, or tax records. Beyond that, lay healers such as Perdomo seldom produced documents that described their work, despite the fact that they administered to far more people than their professional counterparts who dominate the historical record. The amount of data available on Perdomo is itself remarkable and indicative of an unusual individual. Libraries and archives throughout Colombia and Ecuador contain testimonials to his healing abilities, countless newspaper articles (both pro and con) on his work, and many leaflets about him that had been posted or handed out on the streets. In addition, Perdomo published a book, *La iglesia católica en presencia del siglo XIX*, that revealed his beliefs about the proper social role of healers and—perhaps more important, in his mind—offered a spiritual defense of the Catholic Church. This abundant historical information attests to the fact that the healer was exceptional. Yet, despite the records that remain, most of his life is undocumented and beyond the reach of the historian. The materials that are available to reconstruct the life and times of Perdomo are defined by his popularity—and by his opponents.

Even the most general details of his life are unknown. The frontispiece to his book presents a rare photograph of him and the notice that he was born on September 29, 1833, in La Plata, Colombia, in the Department of Tolima. A summary of his baptismal papers indicated that he was the natural son of Concepción Perdomo, but no father is listed. Most children of that era were born to couples who chose not to wed, often because of the high costs associated with marriage sanctioned by the Church; baptismal records in such cases would not list the father. We do know, however, that Francisco Javier Elvira and his wife, Bárbara de la Manjarrez, served as his godparents. Of Perdomo's appearance, descriptions are few, but an 1872 letter described him as follows: "of medium build, of stout frame, with agile movements and agreeable gestures. His complexion is brown . . ; he has black hair, a mustache and goatee; his eyes are vivid, sweet, and expressive; his nose is more small than large and is slightly curved; his teeth are perfect, and he has an agreeable presence and nice voice."[3] We know little of his life before the early 1860s, although he likely practiced medicine as an empiric. Considerable information exists only for the 1867–1874 period. In the 1860s, Perdomo married María Josefa Sánchez and fathered two sons and a daughter. One son, Julio, died in 1874 at the age of eleven, and the other died in 1875 at less than six months of age. María Josefa de Jesús Perdomo, his daughter, lived until at least 1881, seven years after her father died on Christmas Eve 1874 in Guayaquil, Ecuador.[4]

Social Strife and the Church

The civil war that ravaged much of southern and western Colombia between 1859 and 1862 appears to have been a turning point in Perdomo's life. This conflict pitted Conservatives, with bases of power in the Cauca and Antioquia regions, against Liberals, who dominated the coast, parts of the Cauca, the Department of Santander, and much of Cundinamarca.[5] The Liberal and Conservative parties had coalesced in the 1840s from groups separated by regionalism and by often profound ideological differences. Liberals joined moderate Conservatives to initiate the Era of Liberal Reform (1845–1865), which reoriented the political, economic, and, to a lesser extent, social character of the nation. Many reform issues had general bipartisan support, including moves toward a more decentralized political structure, formal statements of political and social rights, expanded suffrage, and the liberalization of economic policies. Reforms that threatened property and socioeconomic structure, including the abolition of slavery, were more divisive. The most bitter and fundamental differences, however, involved the relationship between Church and state and the appropriate foundation of social order—religion or law. The eventual Liberal victory led to the "Radical" Constitution of 1863, which imposed a strict federalist structure upon the nation, purged most remaining vestiges of the colonial Church-state relationship, and completed the liberalization of state economic policies.[6]

Although the Constitution of 1863 had articulated the laws that would guide the country, it by no means resolved the core issues of the era. The armed conflicts of 1876–77, 1883–1886, and 1899–1903, together with the strife of 1839–1842, 1851, 1854, and 1859–1862, made civil war an overwhelming feature of nineteenth-century Colombia. Although nonideological partisan struggles caused many conflicts, the perennial disputes dealt with how the fabric of the colonial order should be rewoven to fit the new nation. Given that the Church was the most powerful colonial institution, that Catholic ideology was the primary foundation of religious beliefs, and that the Church served as the guardian of social order, the construction of the postcolonial state put the Church at the center of most conflicts.

The secularization of society and of political culture divided not only Colombian politics but also most of Western culture. Rationalism, the scientific revolution, and the Enlightenment, the most basic themes of the seventeenth- and eighteenth-century Western world, all undermined the power and function of the once hegemonic Catholic Church. Most ideological disputes were associated with this process. Medicine and healing put the supporters of the Church and proponents of scientific rationalism squarely at odds. The contention that accompanied Perdomo was centered on these ideological differences.

Perdomo claimed a Conservative political affiliation, and his book mounted an unfettered attack on Liberal anticlericalism and the secularization of society. He claimed that the Liberal agenda lacked moral order, which he countered by an extended presentation of the positive role of the Church in society. When Conservatives led the insurrection of 1859, Perdomo joined in the military campaign against the Liberals, serving in the Conservative army under the command of Col. Julio Arboleda. His medical skills reportedly came to Arboleda's attention, whereupon he was assigned to the army's field hospital. The brutal fighting offered him abundant opportunities to expand his medical experience, especially his surgical skills,[7] but the conditions under which he attempted to treat casualties often led to more deaths than did the conflict itself. Wartime deprivations, a lack of supplies, and the limited number of physicians apparently traumatized Perdomo, who later said that he fled the conflict after Arboleda's death on November 13, 1862.

In the wake of the Liberal victory, Perdomo sought refuge with an indigenous tribe in Caquetá, for reasons unknown. He stayed with these people some time; married María Josefa, a member of the community; and learned many of its medical secrets. In particular, he discovered two potent drugs that became the mainstays of his medical kit—a purgative that he called *el toro* (the bull), and *la chispa* (the spark), a powerful emetic. These treatments fit neatly within the treatment methodologies of humoralism, suggesting that even though Perdomo might have used so-called Indian drugs, he did so as part of the Hispanic healing ideology. His stimulants and depressants have been described as "more powerful than those now in use" in Hispanic pharmacies.[8] Other drugs reportedly enabled him to perform operations with little loss of blood, without inflammation, and with reduced pain, results that distinguished him from other surgeons, both lay and professional. Several reports suggest that Perdomo's "internship" in Caquetá heightened his reputation as a healer. From an early date many Hispanics believed that indigenous healers had special powers that they themselves did not possess—powers generally attributed to a perceived association with the devil.[9] The secrets of the natural world, especially of the rain forest, were enviously sought by Hispanics who desired to tame nature and put it to "civilized" use. It is quite possible that such unknown powers were associated with Perdomo, although his rationalist critics made more frequent reference to these powers than did his patients.

If the use of indigenous drugs heightened Perdomo's abilities, his showmanship amplified the impact of those drugs. For example, Perdomo is known to have played a trick on the visitor to his office, wherein he would crush a leaf and have the person breathe in deeply of its vapor, promptly causing a violent nosebleed. The frightened visitor, seeking relief, was then told to inhale the odor of another leaf, whereupon the bleeding would "miraculously" stop.[10] This leaf was probably from the *perro* tree, which Perdomo related had the power both to start and stop nosebleeds when prepared differently. The *perro* leaf also seems to have been his means of stopping bleeding during surgery, which, as mentioned, was a source of much of the acclaim that accompanied his operations.[11]

Perdomo also used humoral medicine. He relied upon *el toro* for a variety of internal illnesses, perhaps to counter a humoral imbalance by the prescription of a "hot and dry" purgative. Testimonials to his healing methods mentioned *el toro* most often, but he employed a wide variety of drugs. For paralysis or nervous attacks, he soaked the roots of the herb *cuarzo* in alcohol for fifteen days. The resulting poultice was then applied to the afflicted parts of the body twice a day, and the patient was advised to stick to a bland diet. A headache was treated with the wood of the "white wax" tree, which was pulverized and applied to the forehead. Irregular menstrual periods were cured by the leaves of the *centella* plant, rolled into pills and swallowed. Perdomo used the vomiting and purging power of *el toro* for the relief of pain, certain intestinal worms, and hemorrhoids. The *toro* tree grew just below the alpine line. He reduced its bark to a fine powder that, when mixed with water, produced a strong and immediate purgative. Its effect could be controlled by drinking a hot tea made from the leaves of the same tree.[12] The most spectacular resource in his medical kit was the drug that he used in his surgeries; many witnesses spoke with amazement of the lack of bleeding or pain in these procedures. Insufficient evidence prevents a detailed analysis of Perdomo's treatment methodology, but extant information suggests to us its humoral character—a healing ideology that helped sustain the Hispanic medical system.

The testimonials of twenty-two people about their treatment at the hands of Perdomo are reproduced in the Appendix. Their ailments varied widely: contracted tendons, breathing problems, fevers, cysts, tumors, and, most frequent of all, vision and urinary problems. Twelve of the patients who visited Perdomo commented that they had been seen by physicians before but without relief. All reported that he had cured them of their afflictions, eight by surgery, four by oral doses, and three by applications of what might have been plasters. A handful reported that his surgery was painless. The testimonials did not cite the names of the various drugs he used, but accounts after 1872 suggest that *el toro* and *la chispa* dominated his pharmaceutical store.

As part of his public persona, Perdomo sometimes volunteered to help a local parish collect money for charity or a building project. And, though his medical skills were akin to those of many empirics, [*curanderos healer*] his refusal to charge for his services was unusual. He noted that he "did not thirst for gold" but healed out of "Christian charity."[13] In fact, Perdomo's Catholicism permeated his healing practices. An observer noted that "the first thing that he does when he approaches the outskirts of a town is to sponsor a festival of the *triduo* [triduum] of the Forty Hours, or spiritual seclusion, in order to lend to his mission the most noble aspects of humanity, so that the physical cures he would effect would come as a natural consequence [of the religious rituals]. . . . Perdomo is placed with a table in front of him, on which are various flasks of drugs, some rusted surgical instruments, and on the near wall an oil painting representing the Sacred Heart of Jesus, made in Quito."[14] Such observations led José María Cordovez Moure to claim that Perdomo practiced a "religious-medical ministry."[15]

Catholic sensibilities shaped the testimonials about Perdomo, especially as they concerned the relationship between healing and charity. When Fermín Rivas Rodríguez expressed his gratitude to the *curandero* for healing his three-year-old daughter of a bladder ailment, he asserted that Perdomo was a compassionate humanitarian dedicated to "those in agony" and "destined by Providence to alleviate the suffering of the poor."[16] (See Document 6 in the Appendix.) A letter with fifty-four signatures praised the *curandero*'s "ardent charity" in helping the "afflicted people" of Serrezuela. (See Document 7.) In thanking God for Perdomo's benevolence, the author of a letter from the "ill and poor of Guaduas" stated that charity demonstrated humanity's worthiness of the divine. It was seen as an act of love and concern for the forgotten, an action that originated not in intellectual progress or material gain but in spiritual progress and knowledge of "the truth." That Perdomo's medicines had been determined to be effective and that he refused to accept money for his services were taken as proof of his "charitable nature."[17]

The Traveling Healer

In 1866, Perdomo left Caquetá and began his healing travels southward into the Ecuadorean highlands. Over the next eight years, he visited scores of towns in Ecuador and Colombia. By 1872, he claimed to have healed in the Provinces of Pichincha and Guayas in Ecuador and throughout the Cauca, Antioquia, Tolima, Cundinamarca, and Santander regions of Colombia.[18] Testimonial letters, newspaper accounts, and other sources reveal that he practiced in Ecuador from 1866 until 1868, in Colombia from 1869 until early 1874, and again in Ecuador in 1874, the year of his death. He usually stayed in a town for only a few weeks, treating the inhabitants of an area in exchange for shelter and sustenance provided by the city council, a local priest, or a partisan supporter.

Perdomo first appeared in the historical record in 1866 due to a series of incidents in Quito, Ecuador. Shortly after his arrival there, *La América Latina* reported him to be a "mysterious man," an "instinctive" physician who "cures only by the inspiration of God and without any medical knowledge." The paper also noted that "he asks no payment for his medicine and happily cures all without haste."[19] Virgilio Parédes Borja suggests that both the poor and rich were amazed by his "astonishing cures," including the leaf trick noted earlier. Perdomo's reputation grew rapidly; in fact, so many people crowded around his hotel that the police were forced to control the throng.[20]

Others expressed distrust of the healer. A few doctors reportedly insisted that he take an examination so that he could practice legally. Perdomo abruptly left Quito, seemingly alienated by their hostility,[21] From Tulcan, he wrote that the "good people" of Quito would protect him from "my gratuitous enemies, who seek to represent me to high society as a man of bad faith."[22] Sixteen physicians rebutted this allegation in a *hoja suelta* (leaflet) on November 10, claiming that since they had not requested that he take an examination, they could not be the cause of his departure. The newspaper editor refused to retreat from his version of the story but suggested that both the physicians and the healer could profit from more conciliatory attitudes.[23]

Sometime before September 1867, Perdomo returned to Quito; and once again, he effected spectacular cures that produced public testimonials. J. Antonio Toledo, for example, wrote that the empiric removed an abscess from his knee that had hampered his movements since 1859; the surgery allowed him to walk without difficulty. Asunción León stated that Perdomo removed a painful tumor from her left eye that local physicians had been unable to cure. And Antonio Múñoz, the parochial judge of Chillagallo, attested that the healer cured various internal disorders through a ten-day treatment with various drugs. Other patients reported cures for nerves, bladder problems, stomach pains, contracted leg tendons, and tumors.[24]

Fermina Cueva was less fortunate—and her experience with Perdomo would have serious repercussions for him. He removed a small tumor from her head, a procedure from which she recovered. However, according to some reports, a sack of wheat fell upon her back while she was at a flour mill, aggravating a liver disorder and forcing her to visit San Juan de Dios hospital, where she died. The police commissioner ordered Perdomo arrested while the cause of her death was investigated. Perdomistas criticized the arrest, claiming that Cueva had not been under the healer's care when she died. Moreover, they argued that professional doctors were not detained when their patients died. Perdomo's arrest, they said, originated in the "ignoble passion of his enemies. . . . The imprisonment of this innocent man and the charge levied against him dishonors his detracters more than it discredits the incarcerated man."[25]

In several leaflets, Perdomistas railed against the unjustness of his confinement. One pamphlet, authored by "Unos reconocidos," claimed that Perdomo offered services to the poor that they could get nowhere else, especially not at the Hospital de Caridad, where professional doctors (and their students) subjected them "to slow and adventurous treatments."[26] Another leaflet criticized that "cursed" law that gave a medical monopoly to university doctors, especially as it was used against Perdomo, who healed the poor without charge.[27] For his part, Perdomo wrote: "I have no other objective than to make several supposed geniuses see that the Supreme Being has not limited the knowledge of nature, nor its special skills, to those who have received academic training. . . . The Glory of God, in His faithful Providence, has chosen me to serve as an instrument of His power, but I am not a doctor graduated from a university, but a coarse and unlettered man."[28]

Some professional doctors disagreed with this portrayal. Several physicians were members of the city council, the agency that had managed the protomedicato since the colonial period.[29] Under municipal statutes, the policing agency was responsible for enforcing public health regulations on the council's behalf.[30] The physicians used their influence on the council to have Perdomo charged with practicing medicine without a license and fined 50 pesos. Since he said he had no money, Perdomo remained in jail.[31] The arrest caused considerable political tension in Quito. Mariano Bustamante, the jefe político (local political boss), urged the council to agree that people such as Perdomo who could not pay large fines and were therefore jailed should be given their freedom so that they could pay their fines in monthly installments.[32] Perdomo's supporters distributed a leaflet entitled "An Undeserved Outrage" on December 5, in which they charged that his "enemies" were manipulating justice.[33] Another leaflet stated that the doctors had "no more principles nor glory than money."[34]

At that point the panel of doctors released the report on the cause of Cueva's death. They concluded that an autopsy had given no indication that Perdomo's operation was in any way connected with the death, as they could detect no lesions on any of the patient's organs.[35] With this finding, the healer was released from confinement. Over two hundred people and a band accompanied him as he left the prison.[36] There remained, however, the matter of the 50-peso fine. One week later, Manuel Tovar, the governor of the province, appealed to the city council to pardon Perdomo "out of respect for the poor of the city, so as to avoid the sacrifices that they will have to make in order to pay for the fine that you have imposed. Perdomo cannot pay for it, because he cured everyone for free, and because of this I have been obliged to take a side in the interest of humanity."[37] The council members protested that only the legislature could grant an exemption to the law—as the governor knew—and affirmed that they would not commit an illegal act, no matter how well-meaning the traveling healer was. Three times the governor insisted; three times the council members refused. They demanded that Perdomo undergo an examination if he wished to continue his medical practice. Instead of complying, the healer left Quito and returned to Colombia. It is unclear whether the fine was ever paid or, if so, by whom.

San Juan de Dios

Perdomo took up residence at his hacienda, San Juan de Dios, upon his return to Colombia. Although his relationship with the Order of San Juan de Dios is unclear, the name he chose for the hacienda suggests that it was a potent influence. The mission of the healing order coincided with Perdomo's own work, and the property was not so much an agricultural venture as part of his healing mission. A small hospital on the estate attracted hundreds of people seeking Perdomo's medical assistance. Leandro M. Pulido, one of that group, reported that residents from Antioquia, Boyacá, Magdalena, Tolima, and Cundinamarca, in addition to people from throughout the Cauca, visited San Juan de Dios. Pulido spoke of hundreds of cures and refuted the observations of some critics who claimed that between 30 and 50 patients died under Perdomo's care. For Pulido, that there were only 50 deaths out of 8,500 treatments was indicative of an astonishingly high success rate, one that compared favorably to a reported 10 percent death rate for the hospitals of Paris.[38]

The limited number of sources that describe this period of Perdomo's life leave much unclear. Property records indicate that he sold a farm north of Popayán in 1869 that was likely part of the San Juan de Dios hacienda, but they do not indicate when he had purchased it; the notarial archives show that he sold this part of his hacienda to Manuel Mosquera for 61 pesos.[39] The property was located in the District of Cajibío, some 28 kilometers north of the city. Although much of the district is mountainous, the terrain around the river is flatter and well suited to cattle grazing, subsistence farming, and other agricultural pursuits.[40] San Juan de Dios seems to have occupied a more favorable location bordered by the *camino real* (royal highway) and the Cofre River. In 1871, Perdomo sold most of the rest of his hacienda to Daniel Valdivieso for the substantial sum of 4,800 pesos. In that transaction, Valdivieso obtained a two-story tiled house, 110 cows, 59 mares, 2 riding horses, and various other farm animals.[41] Two other parcels, seemingly the rest of the property, were sold to neighbors Dionisio León and Antonio Mosquera in the same year.[42]

Perdomo had obviously become a man of relative financial wealth, although just how he attained that status is unclear. The reported value of San Juan de Dios at the time of sale was 2,500 pesos, making it the fourth most valuable property among the ninety-six listed in the district by the notarial official that year. (The average value of these properties was 763 pesos.[43]) In 1881, seven years after Perdomo's death, María Josefa Sánchez, his wife, registered his will and legalized her inheritance. The Perdomo estate, valued at 11,046.20 pesos, included two houses in Popayán, a one-story house on the Calle Chirimoyo, and a two-story house on the Calle de Comercio. The estate also included 11 horses, 16 cows, 1 "fine" mule, and 9 "ordinary" ones. His wife (who had remarried, to Francisco Arjona Sánchez) and minor daughter, María Josefa de Jesús Perdomo, shared the estate equally.[44]

Critics of Perdomo suggested one means whereby he might have acquired his moderate wealth. During a visit to the Santander region in 1873, "L. R. S." recounted that perhaps one-fourth or at least one-eighth of the healer's 4,000 visitors paid 2 pesos to his secretary for prescriptions. Given the length of time that Perdomo had spent in Santander, the numbers of patients that he treated, and this rate of income, L. R. S. hypothesized that the healer could earn up to 4,800 pesos every year, an enormous sum for the period. (Daily wages at the time ranged between 1.5 and 3 pesos for unskilled and semiskilled laborers.[45]) The veracity of this report cannot be determined, but in the absence of other indications as to how Perdomo acquired his wealth, the extremely lucrative nature of his healing must be taken seriously. Although most accounts insist that he did not charge for his services, it is very likely that he received generous donations from grateful patients. No one spoke of paying for medicine, but accusations that Perdomo accepted payments should not be dismissed as simple political mudslinging. Perdomo obviously became quite wealthy through his labors as a healer, despite the charitable nature of his work.

Colombian Travels and Troubles

In January 1869, Perdomo left San Juan de Dios, making his way into the northern Cauca. Reports place him in Manizales in May.[46] He continued into Tolima, where he arrived in Neiva in late July. Neiva appears to have been a Liberal stronghold, for he was immediately greeted with hostility from several sectors. Posters called for the "death of the impostor, the father of the *godos*,[47] the discreditor of the doctors, the ruin of the pharmacies [and] a witch." Late on the evening of July 20, Colombian Independence Day, Perdomo returned to his residence. While looking out the window, he heard a voice call out, "Miguel Perdomo, I have left a letter for you at the door." As he opened the door, someone shot him in his right side. Both his supporters and detractors accompanied the *curandero* to the house of Francisco Javier Lasprilla, where he was attended to by a priest. Although seriously wounded, he recovered without incident.[48] From Neiva, he returned to San Juan de Dios.

Perdomo stayed at his hacienda for most of 1870. After the sale of his property was concluded, he traveled northward toward Medellín in September. Reports of miraculous cures followed him wherever he went. Benito Jaramillo García noted that the "magic knife of Perdomo" had been talked about for several years and that its appearance in town had enlivened the populace. Scores of people sought out his services, which Jaramillo called "a favor from Heaven."[49]

Antioquia and its capital of Medellín were Conservative bases, offering an environment in which Perdomo encountered little apparent opposition. In fact, he was welcomed into Medellín by a group of notables, including two members of the state supreme court.[50] He stayed there for several months, publishing *La iglesia católica en presencia del siglo XIX* with the authority and blessing of the archbishop. Half of the book consists of his overview of the Church, including a chapter on how its moral principles should guide human relations. In the volume, Perdomo not only related his ideology of healing, which was firmly rooted in Catholic ideology, but also briefly discussed the plants that he used in his medical practices; the text of scores of handouts and testimonials about his healing abilities were also included. A second edition of the book, incorporating additional testimonials, was published in Bogotá in 1872. The *curandero* moved into the lowland region around Ambalema during early 1872, spending about two weeks each in Lerida, Ambalema, Guaduas, Villeta, and Serrezuela (now Madrid). One account suggested that this route and his visit to Bogotá were part of his pilgrimage to keep a promise he had made to Nuestra Señora de Chiquinquira, herself a healer.[51]

Nuestra Señora de Chiquinquira originated as an image of the Virgin of the Rosary that had been painted on a wooden tablet. During the 1550s her image watched over the home of a Boyacense family in the town of Chiquinquira. Time dulled the luster of the painting, but on December 26, 1586, a servant girl said she saw the Virgin cause the tablet to rise into the air, glow, and regain its initial splendor. The tablet reportedly remained suspended for several days, during which time pilgrims sought the Virgin's assistance. She was believed to have effected several cures during this period and even more in the years that followed and to have rid Tunja of a pestilence in 1588. These powers earned the Virgin widespread acclaim and brought countless pilgrims to her Boyacá home.[52] The Virgin has increased in prominence over the years, coming to serve as a national symbol (she was named patroness of the country in 1919),[53] much as the Virgin of Guadalupe does in Mexico.

"The Applause of the Masses and the Ire of the Professional Doctors"

The first clear public indication that Perdomo's fame had reached the Colombian capital came in the form of testimonials on his curative powers. The newspaper *La Ilustración*, edited by Conservatives Manuel María Madiedo and Nicolás Pontón, published the first such accounts in April 1872.[54] One article, attributed to the "homeless and ill" of Guaduas, claimed that Perdomo had treated some 1,200 people during his mid-March visit to that town. The healer's virtues reportedly included not only his free treatment of the ill and his effective surgery but also the "simple way in which he treated people": "he does not use [complex] terms nor make a distinction between the rich and poor."[55] Many clerics healed for free as a part of their religious mission, but private *médicos* and empirics generally charged for their services. Patients accustomed to charitable medical care often objected to paying fees, especially when treatments were ineffective. It is not surprising, then, that Perdomo's gratuitous services "animated" the populace of the towns he visited. At least a dozen other testimonials on his behalf were published in the capital in the next two months.[56]

An insightful letter describing Perdomo's visit to Serrezuela foreshadowed many of the tensions that would be generated by his stay in Bogotá. The chronicler related that the morning after the healer's arrival, the normally quiet town took on a "curious" air, with the streets "inundated with people." A crowd of armed supporters accompanied Perdomo through the largely Conservative town, motivated by a rumor that the Liberal governor had dispatched an armed force to arrest the *curandero*. From the pulpit Serrezuela's priest welcomed the "good Catholic doctor" who had pledged to pay for a special religious service.[57] After the triduum, Perdomo treated between 300 and 400 patients per day, most frequently using *el toro* (in various concentrations) but also *la chispa*, *el trueno* (the explosion), and *el calmante* (the tranquilizer). He conducted various surgeries, removing cysts, repairing hernias, and extracting one tumor "the size of a hen's egg" from beneath a woman's tongue. The chronicle noted no ill effects of Perdomo's interventions but cautioned that "it might be an appropriate occasion to begin an assessment of the aptitudes and deficiencies of Mr. Perdomo; but it should not be me, a simple chronicler, who involves himself in such matters. . . . It would be very desirable for the distinguished members of the [medical] profession who reside in Bogotá to admit him with benevolence as a countryman who, although of humble birth and without an academic background, has been able to acquire a sizable reputation through methods that are beyond reproach."[58] Professional doctors in Bogotá accepted this challenge.

The *curandero* arrived in Bogotá on April 29. He initially took up residence with Nicolás Pontón, though the demand for his services forced him to move to a larger location.[59] Perdomo did not attempt to cure all of the hundreds who sought his assistance. An observer noted that he would first conduct a brief examination of the supplicant to determine if he could effect a cure. If he thought he could, he then undertook the cure without charge.[60] Among his early patients were Antonio María Amézquita and León Ortiz, upon whom he performed operations.[61] Several sources indicate that Perdomo became "the talk of the town" and the topic of unending conversation. On the streets, he was surrounded by admiring crowds, many of whom contrasted his positive attributes with the negative qualities of Bogotá's own medical community. Some called him the "people's doctor," the "prophet," and even the "new messiah."[62]

Perdomo had arrived in Bogotá at a particularly important time in Colombian medical history. After the long colonial period, during which formal medicine had been dominated by the Catholic Church, physicians had taken steps to institutionalize a secularized, scientific medical system in the Colombian capital. They had been handicapped by the liberal Law of 1850, which permitted any person to practice a profession without formal training. Leading physicians had opposed that law and had struggled through the 1850s to establish a medical school. Finally, in 1867, they gained legislative approval for the inclusion of a medical school in the newly founded Universidad Nacional. Directors of the medical school also gained control over the largest hospital of the city, through which they attempted to inculcate medical practices common in Europe. Perdomo represented a challenge to these "advances"—a challenge that professional physicians met with concerted action.

Several physicians signaled their antagonism toward the *curandero* in a publicly circulated letter dated May 4. They claimed that two doctors, José María Buendía and Antonio Vargas Reyes, had requested that Perdomo exhibit his surgical skills at the Hospital de Caridad so that Buendía might assess his abilities. The letter's authors welcomed the invitation insofar as it would allow the "truths" of Perdomo's secrets and procedures to become known. They contended that the healer could demonstrate his honor by accepting the invitation, which they said was motivated by nothing other than the search for "truth, the foundation of science"—a search that could only benefit "science and humanity." The *curandero* was invited to bring "two or more professors or gentlemen of his choice" to observe the examination.[63]

Perdomo immediately wrote the editor of *El Diario de Cundinamarca* that he had received no such invitation. Further, he denied having "the honor of knowing these gentlemen," suggesting that he had been too busy to read the newspaper, as he had been working from five in the morning until nine at night. Indeed, he claimed to have seen 2,318 people between April 30 and May 8. Given this onerous schedule, the healer professed to have no time to visit the hospital, but he invited Buendía, Vargas Reyes, or Pedro Navas Azuero, the hospital's director, to visit him at their leisure and observe him at work.[64]

The volatility of the city's populace soon became apparent. On May 5, Francisco Toledo, an empiric working in the central plaza of the city, administered a drink to an invalid, causing him to become quite ill and die. One report suggested that Toledo, by his act, had intentionally satirized Perdomo in hopes of discrediting the *curandero* in the public eye. Another asserted that Toledo had tried to pass himself off as an assistant to the doctor, to the same end.[65] Still others suspected a plot by medical students to undermine support for Perdomo. In any case, this incident became part of the growing controversy that surrounded the *curandero*.

Three days later, Manuel María Madiedo analyzed Perdomo's visit in a front-page article in *La Ilustración*. Public opinion, the Conservative commentator observed, was sharply divided. For some, Perdomo was considered a wise man, a wizard, a man of Providence, or even a demigod. Critics ridiculed these sentiments. For them, Perdomo was nothing more than a demonic, audacious charlatan. Others guarded their opinions, waiting for more information. Madiedo agreed with the latter, lamenting that Bogotá had become divided between "the applause of the masses and the ire of the professional doctors." Although he acknowledged that much remained to be determined, he was sure that Perdomo possessed important anesthetic and homeostatic knowledge that merited further inquiry.

Anticipating the core of the ideological confrontation that swelled around the healer, Madiedo insisted that some people "were in love with their own science" and only believed "that which they know themselves." Yet, he pointed out, Perdomo's abilities had been openly demonstrated "like [those of] the barbers of Athens" and could not be doubted. If the healer had discovered a "diamond" of medical knowledge, he thought that the medical community had an obligation to test its validity. Madiedo argued: "If Mr. Perdomo really possesses a secret, even half a secret, but enough to revolutionize the medical therapy, who are we to offend him, to anger him, to irritate him? Our professors should approach this man, this poor man of the people, whom the people believe and love."[66] He concluded that whatever the outcome, an investigation must be made to determine if an obscure Colombian "had added a line of light to the immortal book of human progress, one that we and our grandchildren might read with pride."[67] (Madiedo himself practiced homeopathic medicine and had engaged in several polemics with members of Bogotá's medical community, a point that I will develop in more detail later.)

The public differences between Perdomo and the professional medical community escalated when three physicians on the staff of the Hospital de Caridad again challenged the *curandero* to demonstrate his skills. Their letter was distributed in leaflet form on May 9.

Vargas Reyes, Librado Rívas, and Buendía invited Perdomo to either visit the hospital or allow them to go to his office so that they could form an opinion of "his ability in so difficult a science": "We don't want to place Mr. Perdomo in the obligation of having to undergo an examination, because we know beforehand that he is ignorant of the structure of the human body, that he knows nothing of the three realms of nature, and that the medical advances of the day are for him problems lost in the darkness of ignorance. We only ask, then, practical proofs from him, but in the light, without circumlocution or mystification."[68] Others commented upon the leaflet's belligerent tone, especially its closing comment: "As for ourselves, we don't fear Perdomo or his followers . . . but wait, scalpels in hand, to demonstrate our own skills."[69]

Among those who sought Perdomo's medical assistance was Tomás Sabogal, a middle-aged man with a giant tumor on his side. On May 11, Perdomo removed the tumor in what some described as a difficult procedure. Those who observed the operation were so impressed by the size of the tumor (Perdomo wrote that it weighed 14 pounds!) that they later paraded it through the streets of the capital, shouting "Long live Perdomo!" "Long live Sabogal!" "Down with physicians!" and "Down with the hospital!" The crowd stopped in front of the *botica* of Vargas Reyes, who, when asked for his opinion of the surgery, responded: "It's a good operation if the patient lives."[70] Sabogal survived the procedure without complications and slept that evening in Perdomo's shop. The next morning, however, he was found dead, with a knife wound in his side.[71] Rumors of Sabogal's death swept through the capital. One account suggested that a young man, caught up in the passions and excitement of the crowd, had, for some reason, killed Sabogal. Another rumor blamed the death on medical students at the hospital. Still others thought that Perdomo or his servant had knifed Sabogal to hide the fact that the surgery had failed.[72] Social tension, fueled by the contradictory rumors, increased throughout the city. Sabogal's body was removed to be autopsied in order to determine the cause of death. Beginning at an early hour, Perdomistas paraded through the streets, crying "Long live Perdomo!" and "Death to the doctors!" Rumors that the healer would be seized and arrested if he accompanied the body to the hospital led to threats of violence if anyone tried to apprehend or harm him. Alcalde Joaquín Martínez Escobar guaranteed his safety, but Perdomo later wrote that he requested that the autopsy be performed in public, perhaps in the central plaza, in order to dampen the crowd's passions and to protect himself. Members of the mob stoned Antonio Vargas Villegas, the young son of Vargas Reyes and himself a physician, as well as the houses of several physicians. Medical students joined the melee, shouting their opposition to "fanatic Perdomistas." Local police tried to quell the disorder but with little success. Finally, about four in the afternoon, Perdomo addressed his supporters, restoring a temporary tranquillity to the city. As the healer went back to his house, many people stayed on to "protect" him.[73]

Violence, however, returned. Confrontations erupted early on Monday, May 13, between Perdomistas and supporters of the local medical community. Some rioters carried firearms, but no blood was shed. The police arrested several demonstrators, taking them to the prison and charging them with treason. Partisan political tension escalated with the turmoil. Perdomo later claimed that he had gone to the presidential palace in search of an assurance that he would be protected but that President Manuel Murillo Toro had refused to see him. Instead, the healer asserted, Murillo had called out four hundred members of the National Guard, who dispersed the crowd with armed force before assaulting Perdomo's house. Some guardsmen, he insisted, gained entrance and stole medical equipment.[74] No doubt shocked by the incident, the *curandero* announced his intention to leave the city, which he appears to have done the next day in the company of forty armed men.[75] Officials of the National Guard denied this account, saying that Perdomo had never requested an audience with the president and that the guards had returned to their barracks when the crowd had broken up.[76] Only the mayor and two members of the police force had entered Perdomo's house, they said.[77]

Although the social upheaval declined in intensity with Perdomo's departure, it took several days for peace to return to the Colombian capital. A crowd "serenaded" Vargas Reyes on Monday night, shouting insults at him for hours. Medical students roamed throughout the city, shouting "Down with the Perdomistas!" and "Down with the fanatics!" Vargas Villegas and another youth, both of whom were armed, threatened a tailor on Tuesday.[78] Doctors Lino Rúiz and Vargas Reyes left Bogotá for Europe on May 18, at least in part to escape the turmoil that they and their families had experienced.[79]

A distinguished body of men witnessed the May 14 autopsy of Sabogal's body. Manuel María Madiedo, the editor of *La Ilustración*, Ricardo de la Parra, Andres María Pardo, Rafael Rocha Castilla, Bernardo Espinosa, and Julio Corredor watched as doctors Abraham Aparicio and Policarpo Pizarro performed the procedure at the San Juan de Dios hospital. Parra and Madiedo were both supporters of Perdomo; the others represented the city's professional medical community. After the autopsy, Aparicio and Pizarro concluded that a hemorrhage resulting from Perdomo's surgery was the "unique and exclusive" cause of death. In their opinion the knife wound, which would not have been fatal, took place after Sabogal had died.[80]

The postmortem on Perdomo's visit was conducted in the press, a far more public and contentious arena. Partisan bickering soon reached conspiratorial levels. Manuel de Jesús Barrera questioned why the body of the man who had been poisoned by Toledo on May 5 had not been autopsied, whereas Sabogal's death had been investigated with appropriate promptness. Did the medical community practice favoritism in the completion of its responsibilities?[81] Supporters of Perdomo asserted that most of the blame for the social unrest lay with the medical community. Underpinning many pro-Perdomo comments was social hostility. Ezequiel Ramírez Moreno, in attesting to Perdomo's cure of his daughter's gallstone, insisted that some doctors were jealous of the *curandero's* success and his following among the poor.[82] A letter from "Q" suggested that certain professional doctors lacked charitable and patriotic sentiments and therefore criticized any possible merit in Perdomo's treatment. He stated: "The fact is that Perdomo is not one of those doctors who advertise in the press that on such and such days they will treat the poor for free, but when a poor person arrives to take advantage of the offer, [he or she finds] that the cost of the prescribed medication also pays for the [allegedly free] consultation. Mr. Perdomo is hardly troublesome to anyone, least of all to the poor, but on the contrary, he helps those with money, and this is the point in question."[83] Indeed, Dioniso Soto asserted that Perdomo's support was rooted in the fact that he was *not* socially eminent and that he was considered a "father of the poor." "The poor people might have lost a great treatment for their pains," he said, and the country had lost a great man. Although Soto did not disparage the virtues of the professional doctors, he indicated that they should not have treated Perdomo so unjustly.[84]

An editor of the Liberal *El Diario de Cundinamarca* joined the analysis of Perdomo. He acknowledged that the healer might have stumbled upon some valuable medical knowledge but argued that if Perdomo did not submit to an investigation, the public and physicians would never truly know. Whatever medical merit the healer might possess, he continued, the violence that accompanied his visit was unacceptable: "What we now see in Bogotá is simply a struggle between good sense and blind ignorance."[85] Unfortunately, another Liberal editor complained, the public disorder threatened the broader peace, and President Murillo's conduct had only exacerbated the issue. Conservative spirits had been animated, the Liberal said, renewing old rivalries. Some Conservatives alleged that Perdomo had been sent by God to improve humanity's plight with the most marvelous and impressive cures. Although the editor did not doubt the loyalty of "the sensible people of the capital," he believed there was cause for concern about others. He mentioned that two meetings had been held, with one group of people heading off to Guasca, the base of an infamous (in the Liberal mind) guerrilla gang during the 1859–1862 civil war. The president had a duty, the writer continued, to act with prudence and responsibility to forestall any threat to the public order.[86]

El Bien Público's editor, who leaned toward the "independent Liberal" perspective,[87] decried the recurrence of public disorder, suggesting that the president bore at least part of the responsibility for the recent turn of events. Rumors grew of a Conservative movement, perhaps headed by Perdomo, as students and Perdomistas continued to roam the streets of Bogotá. Public authorities said they had taken precautions, but the writer noted derisively that these steps consisted mainly of ordering the guards to remain in their barracks and protect themselves against possible harm. Meanwhile, "some members of Congress [had] armed themselves to the teeth" to protect their homes against the wrath of the crowd. The editor doubted that all the rumors were false, suggesting that the tension reminded him of the period of social conflict in June 1853 or of the months before the coup by Gen. José María Melo in April 1854. He asked who stood to gain the most from the upheaval—President Murillo, pseudo-Conservatives who had taken up the Perdomista banner, or pseudo-Liberals who wanted to overthrow the state government?

Whatever the answer, he said, citizens had to look after their own welfare because the state government was impotent and lacked influence and because the national government was purely defensive. He also wrote that the crowd supposedly had stationed itself near the presidential palace, shouting "Long live Perdomo!" and "Long live President Murillo!" Although he made it clear that he did not perceive a common cause between the president and Perdomo, he also pointed out that both men were idolized by a part of Bogotá's populace that merited close attention from partisans of order.[88] Like the Liberal editor, this writer called attention to the apparent linkages between President Murillo, the revived Democratic Society, and Conservative Perdomistas.[89]

Evidence exists to suggest the plausibility of the last accusation. Bogotá's artisans, potent political actors since the 1840s, had recently revitalized the Democratic Society, an organization that had supported widespread popular political activities in the 1850s as well as the Melo coup.[90] A meeting of the artisans at the Institute of Arts and Trades was attended by numerous Liberals, including some of the medical students who had been active in the recent disturbances. Other artisans waited outside the meeting place, dismayed at the Liberal influence over the gathering. Eventually the artisans drifted away from the meeting, seemingly alienated by the students. Medardo Rivas (who later penned the bitter critique of Perdomo cited in Chapter 2) urged the artisans to remain, but the meeting continued with only leading Liberals and students in attendance. "Caputso," the author of an article on this event, criticized the whole affair as a farce, especially since Liberals had applauded the state and local governments but had "used the stick on Bogotá's Perdomistas" just a few days earlier. Caputso congratulated the "real" artisans for safeguarding themselves against political exploitation.[91]

As Perdomo prepared to leave Bogotá, he wrote an explanatory letter to the editor of *La Ilustración* in which he addressed "the true people of Colombia." The "patient and laboring masses" who carried the burden of the nation received few benefits for their labor, he wrote. He complained of his treatment in the capital but confessed that he had known beforehand that "professors of medicine" had opposed his visit; indeed, their opposition in part motivated that visit, for he wanted to demonstrate to them that he had learned of certain drugs that might positively affect the healing practices. He noted that, though most Bogotanos accepted and appreciated his medical treatments—as others had elsewhere over the previous ten years—the professional community and Liberal authorities solidly opposed him because he was a Conservative and because his medical practices differed from theirs. Perdomo charged that a conspiracy aimed at undermining his public support had instigated most of the violence, symbolic of the attitudes that many Colombian authorities held toward the people. He found it most appalling that "these insults have come from precisely the same people who have an obligation to demonstrate their civility and benevolence, toward me perhaps, but certainly toward the people; in all instances the doctors, intellectuals, and students should be the model of decorum, as should the authorities and magistrates who represent the law and public morality; they should be the mirror that reflects society and its educational structure."[92]

Protesting his innocence in the death of Sabogal, Perdomo declared that he was at peace with God and with the truth. His singular goal, he said, was to help heal people using the drugs that he had acquired in Caquetá. He had once hoped that Bogotá's professors might have helped him explore their qualities, but now he insisted that he intended to travel to Europe, where "truly competent scientists" could assist him.[93] Regarding those who called him a charlatan, Perdomo said that others would be the judge. He acknowledged that he had no formal medical training, nor was he aware of the latest scientific discoveries. He did, however, claim tremendous practical experience, as demonstrated by his abilities in a variety of complex surgeries. How, he asked, could he be such a quack when he had treated over two hundred thousand people? Those people were his rightful judges: if they had found him guilty, they would not have sought his help. Perdomo insisted that his critics were motivated not by a concern for his medical abilities but by political and professional antipathies. They refused to acknowledge that a "poor and simple man of the people" could have been favored by God with the knowledge of "some natural forces that were until now unknown to science."[94]

As Bogotá returned to normal in the wake of Perdomo's visit, some resentments lingered. Caputso noted that the autopsy on Sabogal, though no doubt accurate, was being manipulated by the medical and judicial communities. He insisted that local authorities were seeking a charge of involuntary manslaughter against Perdomo that would "leave the doctors in peace and pacify their positions as *sabios* [wise men]." This stance was absurd, the editorialist asserted: deaths from surgeries were all too common and never resulted in criminal charges. Moreover, he pointed out, Francisco Toledo, who had poisoned the invalid in early May, had been promptly released without charges and had been allowed to leave the city.[95] "We request," he wrote, "that the Chief Justice of the State proceed with impartiality and with rectitude in this case, keeping in mind that Dr. Miguel Perdomo is a cause of the people; that *the question is not a political one*, but a question of great interest for society, not only for Colombia, but for all of humanity in that an enraged public has never been stilled by force of arms."[96]

The legal charges against Perdomo slowly made their way through the judicial system. Given that the national laws allowing for the free practice of professions had removed medical doctors from legal oversight, the state prosecutor determined the death of the *curandero*'s ill-fated patient to be accidental. The state's Superior Court, however, reversed this ruling, finding that Perdomo was indeed responsible for Sabogal's death. The penal code stated that one who "by a cause that he could or should be able to avoid, or who has, even involuntarily, caused a death, should suffer imprisonment for between six months and two years." Even though the constitution allowed for the free practice of a profession, the court found, Perdomo should have known the rules of medicine governing surgery and must be held responsible for upholding them. Professional training assured knowledge of medical rules, and if Perdomo undertook an operation beyond his capability or knowledge and in ignorance of science, he could cause a death that otherwise might have been avoided. The court therefore charged him with homicide and ordered his arrest.[97]

Perdomo, of course, was no longer in the capital, though he remained in central Colombia after his departure from Bogotá. He apparently stayed at the hacienda "El Riachuelo," near Serrezuela, for several weeks in fear of legal retribution (according to Cordovez Moure). Soon, he renewed his travels, visiting Puente Grande, El Cerrito, Mosquera, and Puerto de Zipaquirá, where he continued to practice his healing.[98] Perhaps he completed his pilgrimage to Chiquinquira, for by April 1873, he reportedly had stayed at Susacon and San Jil, both in the State of Santander to the north of the holy site.[99] In all probability, he resided in Mompos in early 1874, for we know that his son Julio died there.[100]

Perdomo returned to Quito in 1874. Once again his surgical skills won him fame, but they also brought on legal problems. He was jailed after a woman upon whom he had operated died. Padre Luis Sodiro, a professor of botany at the Escuela Politécnico, helped him gain his freedom in exchange for information about the plants he used in his practice, one of which was known as *alizá*.[101] Perdomo left shortly thereafter for the port of Guayaquil, where he set up shop to treat the scores of people seeking his assistance. Mauro Madero cites four notable surgeries performed by the healer in Guayaquil: the removal of tumors from a breast, a wrist, and an eye and the excision of a growth from a child's nose.[102]

While treating a young man's illness, Perdomo contracted a disease, perhaps smallpox or yellow fever.[103] The *curandero* sickened rapidly, dying early on December 24, about a month after having arrived in Guayaquil. When an angry crowd threatened to sacrifice the youth who had "caused" the death of the messiah, the young man sought and found refuge with Perdomo's wife. After the *curandero*'s death, rumors spread throughout the city that his grave had been found open and that some people had seen him walking on the road to Quito, a clear allusion to his Christ-like character. Others claimed that his body had been stolen. One reporter investigating the story approached the police, who said they found that a body near Perdomo's had been moved, although the reporter doubted that the populace would believe that account.[104] Perdomo's reputation persisted in Guayaquil well into the twentieth century—a testimony to his intense popularity.

4

THE EMERGENCE OF MEDICAL PLURALISM

Sickness is central to the human condition, for we all suffer through illnesses from which others help us recover. Our episodes with ill health create a shared experience that facilitates the study of other peoples in the present and in the past. Yet insofar as the diseases and processes that restore health are defined by culture, different people understand illness and methods of healing in different ways. Thus, what was once known as leprosy has come to be known as Hansen's disease,[1] and what is called epilepsy by some is called *qaug dab peg* (the spirit catches you and you fall down) by others.[2] The cultural foundation of healing imposes a warning: An understanding of medicine should not be transferred simplistically from one culture (or time) to another. Although the centrality of healing empowers our capacity to reflect upon the lives of others, that reflection threatens to project the ideologies, values, and constructions of our own medical system(s) onto our reading of others. Medical systems differ markedly among distinct cultures, and some societies use multiple systems of medicine to cure distinct illnesses. Medical pluralism seems more prevalent in regions of the world characterized by abrupt cultural encounters or by an extended colonial experience. People within these societies have a greater capacity to utilize multiple approaches to healing.

I tend to doubt that one can truly understand a medical system other than one's own. This inability to remove indigenous cultural blinders is compounded by distance in time. At best the historian can document an earlier culture's apparent characteristics, demonstrate the historical forces that shaped it, and attempt to analyze it. But at the end of the day, one may well be more confident of the narrative presentation than of historical truth. Such projects are nevertheless interesting, and they are valuable because of the insights they offer on our own ways of thinking.

Medical Ideologies in the Great Transformation

Contemporary Latin America is a medically pluralist region. However, the labels that scholars apply to the multiple medical systems now in operation vary. Virginia Gutiérrez de Pineda, writing about Colombia, notes the presence of two generalized systems, "one oriented toward the academy and the other toward popular knowledge and practices." She labels the former system *medicina facultativa* (academic medicine) and the latter *medicina tradicional* (traditional medicine).[3] Carlos Viesca Treviño distinguishes between traditional and popular medicine in Mexico. In his sense, popular medicine is akin to household medicine, which is passed along socially without a formally elaborated system. Traditional medicine, modified by the passage of time and the influence of scientific medicine, is rooted in pre-Columbian and Hippocratic-Galenic practices and is generally associated with *curanderismo*.[4] In regard to Venezuela, Jacqueline Clarac de Briceño identifies two conglomerated medical systems, a popular/traditional system with rural and urban dimensions and a Western system that combines naturalist, homeopathic, scientific, and allopathic practices. She finds that a mixture of Spanish, African, Afro-American, and indigenous beliefs sustain the popular/traditional system, a mixture that was largely completed by the end of the nineteenth century.[5] Gutiérrez de Pineda and others agree with Clarac de Briceño that popular/traditional medicine represents the fusion, or at least the interaction, of Hispanic, African, and indigenous systems prior to the nineteenth-century appearance of scientific medicine. In a broader context, Arthur Kleinman identifies at least three overlapping systems of medical beliefs: "The popular sector consists of individual, family, and community beliefs and activities; the folk sector consists of the beliefs and activities of the non-bureaucratic and non-professional healing specialists, including shamans, herbalists, midwives, and bone-setters; and the professional sector consists of the beliefs and activities of the organized and legalized healing professions."[6]

These authors agree that the nineteenth century was a critical era in the formation of the medical pluralism of contemporary Latin America. The establishment of scientific medicine in the Americas and how it became an accepted healing ideology is often described but seldom in the context of existing medical beliefs. The lack of attention to the interaction of medical systems in the 1800s tends to empower scientific medicine and its "rightful" social authority while denying the integrity and presence of other medical beliefs.

The case of Miguel Perdomo Neira offers many insights into an important period in the history of medicine. After many years of relative stability, the Hispanic medical system was exposed to transformative pressures that, in time, would create the medical pluralism of contemporary Latin America.[7] In simple terms this period of transition juxtaposed a Catholic-influenced set of beliefs that drew upon humoral principles and an emerging secular, scientific system that envisioned the body as a knowable machine whose maladies could be corrected. In the colonial era, healing had been a highly social activity, with medical knowledge diffused through large segments of the population. After the nineteenth century, this knowledge became the privileged domain of the few professionals trained in scientific medicine. In earlier times, healing and spirituality had been intimately linked; Perdomo's attitudes toward healing, for example, were inseparable from his Christian sensibilities. The new ideology of rationalism and scientific medicine separated the profane and spiritual domains. In addition, the colonial authorities and structures paled in comparison to the institutions, associations, structures, and legal authority that would be erected around scientific medicine. For all these reasons the ideological contentions of the nineteenth century were necessarily intense, and profoundly different ways of viewing the world sparked the social, political, and theoretical conflicts that characterized the Great Transformation.

Truths in Conflict

Ideologies of healing are so fundamental to cultural artifices as to be cast as truth. Hispanic medicine posited religious and humoral explanations for diseases that afflicted humans, but scientific medical beliefs attributed disease to malfunctions of the biological machine. These new medical beliefs were part of the larger rationalist understanding of the world that formed the backbone of the Enlightenment. Proponents of the new system, such as Charles Stuart Cochrane, a visitor to Colombia in the 1820s, insisted that vestiges of earlier beliefs and practices needed to be cleared away to allow for the progress promised by rationalist thought. Cochrane expressed little tolerance for the colonial social environment. In Bogotá, he observed that

> there are nine monasteries for men, and three convents for women; the others have fallen into decay as a consequence of the revolution, and from the increase of knowledge and penetration of the natives, who are fast throwing off the yoke of bigotry and priestcraft and assuming the right of man to think and act for himself. A considerable number of these sluggish priests are, however, still left to fatten on the plunder which they extract from the credulity of the populace, though it is to be hoped that the march of human intelligence in the transatlantic world will not be long delayed by such drones, but that a short time will bring their total dispersion.[8]

Advocates of scientific medicine saw themselves as progressives who, along with others of their kind, would purge Latin American societies of their colonial characteristics, most notably the pervasive ideological and institutional influences of the Church. In promulgating scientific medicine, they broached the divisive question of the proper role of religion in society or, put differently, the proper degree to which society should be secularized. Liberal anticlerics attempted to eliminate all institutional authority of the Church; many wished to reduce its social power as well. These advocates for change encountered strong resistance, in part because of the deeply Catholic nature of Andean society. Perdomo's supporters used the language of Christian charity to express their gratitude and their ideology of healing. His scientific opponents used the authority of science to level a rationalist critique against him. Scientists and scientific physicians thought of themselves as "workers of progress" who labored to construct the "edifice of scientific emancipation."[9] As Manuel Uribe Angel states, "The discovery of the truth, then, is the objective of science, the noble and eternal aspiration of rational beings and the precise foundation upon which the civilized world works."[10]

The campaign to secularize Latin American society was a major dimension of the modernization of the region—a complex process whose primary features, though disputed, implied, at the least, the transformation of the area's politics, economics, beliefs, and social structures. Scientific medicine was intimately connected with the process of exerting powerful influences upon existing systems. "There is indeed a sense in which all modern medicine is engaged in a colonizing process. . . . It can be seen in the increasing professionalization of medicine and the exclusion of 'folk' practitioners, in the close and often symbiotic relationship between medicine and the modern state, and in the far-reaching claims made by medical science for its ability to prevent, control, and even eradicate human diseases."[11]

The modern intellectual tendencies of deism, materialism, Marxism, anarchism, liberalism, and positivism imagined humans to be purely secular beings, conceptions that clashed with traditional Catholic and Protestant beliefs. Consequently, the Great Transformation produced social tensions in many aspects of life. Sometimes these tensions erupted into rebellion, as happened in the backlands of Brazil,[12] as well as the region around Tomochic, Mexico.[13] Intellectual movements such as New England's spiritualism and Mexico's spiritism originated in this increasing secularization of temporal life.[14] In Colombia the split between those who believed that God played an active role in the everyday world and those who envisioned the rule of natural law lay at the core of the differences between Perdomo and advocates of scientific medicine.

Proponents of scientific medicine differed on this point as well. Mechanistic interpreters of the body dominated scientific medicine, but homeopathic physicians relied upon the vital force of the anima in their healing ideology. Founders of homeopathic medicine in Colombia, it will be recalled, expressed their support for Perdomo in the 1870s, perhaps because, a decade earlier, they had engaged in a series of heated public exchanges with allopathic physicians.[15] Manuel María

Madiedo's 1863 homage to Samuel Hahnemann included a bitter criticism of allopaths, whose treatment—purges, emetics, and plasters—were, he alleged, dangerous. He contended that the treatments of homeopaths were much safer, in part because fewer and less powerful drugs were used: "The popularity that allopathic medicine has enjoyed until now has been popularity born of monopoly. A system so repugnant, so painful, so dangerous, and so *costly* cannot be naturally popular."[16]

The rector of the medical school, Antonio Vargas Reyes, acknowledged that Madiedo spoke well of philosophy and the abstract sciences. Nonetheless, he said, the man knew very little of science, an understanding that could only come from years of study.[17] Vicente María Reyes, the son of the *Gaceta*'s editor, attacked homeopathy on several grounds. Homeopathy was not a science but "medical heresy," he declared, and its treatment methodology was ineffective because it was unscientific. Both Vicente and his father accused homeopaths of being charlatans who should not be allowed to take their medical practices into the Hospital de Caridad.[18] Indeed, homeopaths were blocked from the hospital as biomedicists sought to make homeopathic medicine illegal.

Madiedo believed that both allopathy and homeopathy were scientific but that they were supported by different philosophies. "Allopathic materialism," he observed, "sees the body as a machine, in which the disease is identified as a problem with organs." Its practitioners "made all of man into a machine, denying that there is any more to it than can be found with the point of a scalpel." By contrast, he said, homeopathy saw changes in organs as phenomena caused by disturbances in the vital force and sought to change those phenomena: "In its effort to rehabilitate the lost harmony [of the vital force], Homeopathy does no more than obey the divine condition, stamped by God on His creations, as a universal revelation for the conservation of His works."[19] Homeopathy as interpreted by Madiedo and Sanmiguel seems to have had far less of the body/mind division of Cartesian dualism than did scientific medicine. It is perhaps not surprising that both men were ardent defenders of Catholicism—and of Perdomo. Interestingly, nowhere in the medical ideology expressed by professors at Bogotá's school of medicine does one find any discussion of the unified body or even of the role of God in healing.

Perdomo wrote that God created nature for the good of humans, who lived within its laws. He believed that humans could discover the secrets of nature as created by God—such as the plants that could combat illness. Thus, he declared, "[my] principles are those of true reason, my knowledge is that of the practical world, and my only book is that of nature." Some people, he wrote, "confuse the power of God with the jurisdiction of the Earth; but if they know the latter, they will know God." For them, rationalism was the answer to natural science, but Perdomo believed "that God is the source of all reason." He asserted that the existence of the natural world was indeed mysterious, with its organisms sustained through the miracles of God.[20] Leandro M. Pulido, an articulate defender of Perdomo, noted that two facets of healing had to be considered, the visible cure and the divine: "If you only take into consideration the first, reason, poor impoverished reason will go from door to door like an impertinent beggar, asking of everyone the explanation of the facts; it will go tired in its pride, when it ought to appeal to faith; in which man can find the divine treasury of all solutions."[21]

Perdomo's ideology was blasphemous to many scientists and liberals. In 1883, Medardo Rivas, one of the era's most potent and prolific Liberal authors, queried whether the healer was a man inspired by God to spread His blessings among the poor and destitute or an impostor who played upon the people's credulity. Rivas thought the latter, and his proof lay in science and rational thought. It was entirely conceivable to him that Perdomo had uncovered medicinal plants whose secrets had been guarded by indigenous peoples. If so, he said, the healer should have earned the gratitude of an appreciative nation, but if he had cloaked knowledge behind claims of mystical powers, should he not be condemned as a fraud?

> The periodicals and publications about Perdomo affirm that he performed surgery with prodigious dexterity, skills that he could not have learned among the Indians; he removed cataracts, which requires a man's lifetime of learning; he extracted cancers, which requires, if it were possible, ability, dexterity, and practice; at the same time he removed goiters, restored

sight and hearing, and alleviated [the suffering] of lepers; for each of these infirmities it would be necessary for him to acquire distinct surprising, marvelous, and extraordinary secrets. Reason rejects, or at least does not understand, that a human mind could embrace such knowledge and be able to recognize infirmities at a glance, and with such ability to perform the most delicate operations; reason cannot comprehend that a man could cure 300 sick people at the same time, [people] with different afflictions, most of them incurable; human reason, in sum, cannot explain what happened with Perdomo.[22]

Having rejected a rational explanation for the *curandero*'s reputation, Rivas suggested that his powers may have been linked to human belief in the marvelous, in the mythical, and in the unexplainable. "These illusions are most fascinating when they offer the fewest guarantees of reality," he said. But after surveying various people with seemingly inexplicable powers, he rebuked them all. Rivas concluded that "the lesson left by Perdomo will remind the people to believe in science, which is the truth, and not allow themselves to be deceived by lies, which are fantasies."[23]

Liberal anticlericalism joined rationalism in rejecting Perdomo's abilities and popularity. The correspondent from the State of Santander known as "L. R. S." penned a revealing critique of the healer in *El Diario de Cundinamarca*, the leading Liberal newspaper of the capital city. He called Perdomo a charlatan and an incompetent physician who passed himself off "as inspired by God who, knowing the credulity and simplicity of the people, has looked for the support of the fanatics." Although L. R. S. acknowledged that Perdomo provided free services, he also pointed out (as mentioned earlier) that the healer accepted donations, probably close to 5,000 pesos per year.[24] L. R. S. suggested that Perdomo, operating without knowledge or skill, seldom stayed in one place for more than two weeks, leaving before his medical shortcomings became widely known—and before his patients realized the unfortunate truth as their illnesses worsened or as they lay dying from his operations. How, then, did L. R. S. explain Perdomo's popularity? He wrote: "The answer is easy: poor people are the same everywhere: simple, credulous, enthusiastic and easily fooled by hallucinations. The people are never bothered by analysis; they admire the impassioned and are always oriented toward the marvelous . . .

[for example] in their belief in the marvelous accounts for their mass pilgrimages to the waters of Lourdes in search of remedies for all their infirmities and cleansing from all their sins."[25] L. R. S. blasted the people's willingness to believe in whichever "mysterious" individual appeared, always supported by members of the Church: "How strange it is that they admire him, that they see in him a mysterious man, approaching on their knees as if he were an altar, with him wearing a priest's collar and always surrounded by priests who have given him their parasitical devotion."[26]

Although scientific rationalism came to dominate the nation's medical and educational institutions, it was not accepted by the bulk of the population. Predictably, Conservatives and others who were closely associated with the Church ardently defended Hispanic beliefs. Sergio Arboleda (1822–1888), the intellectual dean of nineteenth-century Colombian conservatism, served as a powerful voice for Christian morality as the necessary foundation for public and private life. In addressing the relationship between science and religion, Arboleda insisted that science was the result of human mental labor and was of necessity founded upon moral laws. He cautioned that those who strayed from moral laws threatened social disorder. In his mind, science per se was a noble practice, but those who loved science without recognizing a higher moral code corrupted its divine foundation. Religious faith, for him, was the necessary base for a "good" science:[27] "Some people say that this cannot be; it is against the laws of nature. Science! There is not a smaller nor more miserable thing than our present-day science, unless perhaps it is these small, proud worms who call themselves learned men."[28]

Perdomo's beliefs paralleled those of Arboleda, especially in terms of the relationship between morality and public life. In *La iglesia católica*, Perdomo blasted Liberal regimes for having abandoned the Church as the moral guardian of the government. He argued that the moral code of the Church provided the proper principles of society, principles that sustained and stabilized government. Liberals, he said, had systematically violated that code and the country's relationship with the Church; moreover, the government had refused to renew the Concordat with the Vatican, had separated the Church from the state, had declared freedom of religion, had removed the taxes that were intended to support the Church, and had persecuted the Church's ministers. For Perdomo these actions represented "pure crimes against God." In liberal principles, he saw the germination of positivism, which came from not knowing God. The lack of morality under liberalism, he declared, produced licentiousness—the freeing of human passions from moral restrictions.[29]

Catholic healing beliefs, as well as the conflict between scientific rationalism without religion and traditional principles, were exemplified in the miracle of Lourdes. The editors of *La Caridad* posed a vexing dilemma for the *señores racionalistas* (rationalist gentlemen) in their article on this subject. According to the editors, in July 1873, Mercedes Tórres of Fusagasugá, Colombia, who had been paralyzed and bedridden, was miraculously cured. Her illness, which doctors had been unable to cure, had become so severe that she had asked for the last rites, which the local priest administered. Shortly thereafter, she drank a few drops of water taken from the spring at Lourdes and within an hour was able to walk without the assistance of a crutch. Since that healing, the account continued, she had enjoyed perfect health.

This case, the editors insisted, presented a troublesome situation for rationalists. "Science," they noted, "is interested in dispelling doubts; and the rationalists had the philosophical obligation to determine if the many witnesses to [this miracle] are reliable; if they are not, they have no right to deny the power of the supernatural." Rationalists had to prove: 1) Was the woman sick as had been assured; or 2) does the water of Lourdes contain some powerful substance that acts immediately to cure the ill whom science has declared incurable and who are in agony? 3) In this case, they have to say what the water contains and how it works; or 4) they must prove that the witnesses are crazy, or bribed, or foolish . . . and that they have been tricked; or frankly confess that this is a supernatural influence caused by God and that Our Virgin of the Immaculate Conception is a great physician who, when she wants, cures with a few drops of water.[30]

Faith, as opposed to the rational understanding of natural processes (itself a matter a faith), served as the cornerstone of Catholic ideology. Proponents of liberalism threatened not only that faith but also the social order rooted in Catholic principles. As one editor wrote,

"The liberal system is based upon Protestant principles that are contradictory and absurd (the independence of humans), in a way that sanctions the most humiliating tyranny, for when humans depart from their shared destiny and instead seek [individualist] goals that are spurious and ignominious, they practice absolute liberty, openly violating the true human liberties found in social life."[31]

From this point of view, liberalism and rationalism were not only bad for society, they were also bad for doctors. Perdomo articulated a moral code for physicians that originated in a Christian-centered set of human relations. For him the "sacred mission of the doctor is charity." A doctor had to recognize that God is the only source of healing, he said, and the doctor who tried to cure without the necessary knowledge or who healed "motivated by the vile interests of money" did a grave injury to his consciousness. According to Perdomo, it was better to do nothing than to attempt an unknown treatment because, in doing so, the doctor might prolong or worsen the misery of a person whose life was given by God. For the *curandero*, it was equally wrong if a doctor asked a higher price than the base value of the drugs he prescribed, if he thought himself better than the rest of humanity, if he delayed in getting to the house of a sick person, or if he refused to give a prescription because the patient could not pay for his services. To Perdomo, these wrongs represented the separation from God and the rule of passions, faults he attributed to many rationalist doctors.[32]

Perdomo's criticism of professional doctors during the last ten years of his life derived from this moral code. His supporters expressed similar sentiments when they compared the *curandero* to other doctors: "We do not intend to criticize our [professional] physicians, but with what we have seen and felt, we are convinced that the science of Hippocrates and Galen is not found in academic titles but in the soul, in the heart, and in philanthropic sentiments united by the happy predisposition to do well and to practice Christian charity."[33] In this moral code lies one explanation for Perdomo's enormous popularity. Healing was integral to the Catholic ideologies and traditions that were deeply entrenched within Andean society. That he was recognized as "the people's doctor" or "the new messiah" speaks to the profound social power of healing.

The Social Power of Healers

Healers have enjoyed widespread social power in Latin America, in large part because of the region's Catholic heritage, which fuses healing and the sacred into an indivisible unity. This fusion is seen in the image of Christ as healer, but it is also present in the lives of countless saints,[34] as well as in apparitions of the Virgin. Catholic sanctification initially tended to be granted to martyrs, but by the end of the first millennium, it was more often awarded to people such as healers who had done good deeds, who had performed miracles, and who, after death, could "intercede before God on behalf of those remaining in the profane world."[35] Folk saints, not officially canonized by the Church but nonetheless held in high popular esteem, were common. Such traditions were transferred to the Indies, where folk saints became a standard dimension of popular religion.[36]

Many folk saints are believed to have healing powers, and "healing cults" exist to sustain the most revered healers. In general terms the broader the region of a healer's social power, the greater the likelihood that he or she will be associated in the public mind with the Catholic sainthood tradition and that healing cults will evolve.[37] The social power of healers might be confined to a particular neighborhood or province; in exceptional cases, it might cross national boundaries to acquire international prestige, as in the case of Santa Teresa.[38] Exceptional healers at the center of cults might be believed to continue to heal after death, responding to prayers by the ill to approach God and effect a cure. These prayers are often accompanied by a variety of rituals, including the lighting of candles, the laying of wreaths, or the recitation of a particular novena of prayers, much as one would ask an official saint for assistance. Folk saints are often reputed to be strangers to a region, of humble social background, who cure and assist the poor in ways that may appear miraculous.[39] Antonio Conselheiro, the messianic leader of the Canudos Rebellion, certainly fit this description.[40]

The tremendous popularity enjoyed by Perdomo and the near devotion shown to him by his supporters indicated his social power. At his death the pilgrimage of people to his grave and the rumors of his awakening from the dead suggested the powerful Catholic ideology of his adherents. At least one account noted that people spoke of his extraordinary powers and visited his tomb for more than a generation after his death. Clearly, Perdomo shared some of the attributes commonly associated with folk saints, including charitable healing. One of his supporters, Ricardo de la Parra, noted that "he dispenses his forces in the name of Him who dispenses the sun, the air, the rain, and all the goods and ills. He does not make an exception of the persons [whom he heals, but] prefers the poor to the rich, the disgraced to the happy. His untiring diligence is greater and more sweet, and more benighted when the victim is more disgraced. He is a man of and for the people, the good of all, the counselor of the disinherited and patient masses; the health of the people is his sole desire. Charity is the fire that animates him, and the love of his fellow man the spirit that vitalizes him."[41] Yet no healing cult developed around his memory, although the northern Andes does support one of the strongest such cults in Latin America.

The healing cult of the Venezuelan doctor José Gregorio Hernández extends through much of the northern Andes. Gregorio Hernández was a pioneer of scientific medicine who studied in both Caracas and Paris before starting his practice in the Venezuelan capital in 1891. He is credited with having founded modern medicine there and having introduced the use of the microscope to the country. He worked tirelessly in a clinic established for the poor, often offering his services gratis. Gregorio Hernández was a pious individual who lived alone, foregoing the pleasures of drink, smoke, or family. He twice attempted to enter religious orders and, having failed, dedicated much of his life to service to God through his medicine. In April 1919 a car, reportedly one of the first in Caracas, struck and killed him as he tried to cross the street to deliver medicine to a poor patient. He was eulogized as a "sainted man" and soon inspired a healing cult that is supported by various miracles.[42] One account describes an encounter with Gregorio Hernández:

> We were neighbors together in the town of Mene Grande and he [a young man] was operated on in his own home. A man and a girl dressed as a nurse appeared, exactly like in the pictures in the tableau. They went to look for a washbowl, cotton, and gauze. The man spoke to him and told him to lie down, and that he would fall into a deep sleep and later feel

well. When he woke, he had been operated on and found a written prescription by the bed. The staff of the Mene Grande hospital examined him; none of them had seen that type of stitch before. They could not explain what had happened.[43]

Gregorio Hernández has been declared "venerable" by the Vatican (the status preceding sainthood), in large part because of the many healing miracles attributed to him.[44] His healing cult extends throughout Venezuela and into Colombia, Panama, and Ecuador. "Santo Gregorio" often appears to people, wearing a dark suit and carrying a medical bag, and heals them either through medicine or surgery. Holy water with curative powers is said to seep from his tomb, and *promesas* (promises or indulgences) with his image are sold outside churches and in *curanderos'* shops. Because the Church has come to claim Gregorio Hernández's powers, his image is displayed on murals, in many homes, and in automobiles. In some areas his healing cult has spiritist ramifications, as in Puerto Tejada's Centro Hospitalario de José Gregorio, where Brother Walter calls upon the doctor's spirit to guide him in his surgical procedures. Indian healers in Putumayo also use Gregorio Hernández's curative powers.[45]

A powerful healing cult also surrounds Costa Rican doctor Ricardo Moreno Cañas. During the early evening of August 23, 1938, a disenchanted patient murdered Moreno Cañas and another physician, Carlos Manuel Echandi, in their San José homes. Costa Rica mourned the deaths, particularly that of Moreno Cañas, who was probably the country's most popular and preeminent physician. A healing cult had developed around him by the 1940s, as vendors began selling *promesas* on cards with the image of the doctor, a prayer, and instructions on how to petition for his assistance. By the 1970s, spiritualists had also incorporated Moreno Cañas into their ceremonies. Many patients reported that the doctor had healed them, sometimes by performing operations. Moreno Cañas is now revered as a "legendary figure who represents tender, sympathetic, respectful, charitable medical care that utilizes the newest, most highly developed scientific knowledge." Images of the doctor are sold along with those of saints, and his name is invoked by both popular and professional healers.[46] Many Argentines hold Madre María (a lay saint) in similar esteem.[47]

In northern Mexico a cult developed around the spiritist José Fidencio Sintora Constantino, popularly known as *el niño Fidencio*, who practiced his healing arts in Espinozo, Nuevo León, in the 1920s and 1930s. Most of his cures involved herbs and humoral treatments, but he also practiced minor surgery. *El niño Fidencio* reported that he had been given curative abilities by a Christ-like bearded man who came to him in a vision. Perdomo and Gregorio Hernández claimed no special powers, but the saliva, breath, and touch of *el niño Fidencio* were said to have curative effects. A powerfully aesthetic individual, he acted as a priest in Espinozo, where he baptized residents. During his life many people treated him as a saint, "kissing his hands, feet, and the hem of his gown." Since his death, his birth and death days have become occasions for major festivals, when hundreds of people flock to Espinozo to visit his tomb, converse with his spirit, or seek his curative assistance. Fidencistas operate throughout northern Mexico and the southwestern United States, serving as mediums so that his devotees might speak with *el niño Fidencio* or seek his cures.[48]

Many of the aforementioned cults attend primarily to the physical aspects of healing. But the Bataque cults of Brazil envision curing somewhat more broadly, addressing the wide array of problems afflicting the quality of life for Brazil's urban poor, not just their illnesses. The Bataque mediums might seek to redress the trauma of family strife, alcoholism, the loss of employment, or problems with a boy- or girlfriend.[49]

These and other healing cults represent the mixture of Afro-American and Catholic religious beliefs and turn-of-the-century spiritism.[50] In some instances healing cults have emerged quite directly from Afro-American traditions, as is seen in the Bataque cults or in the voodoo practices of Haiti. In other cases, cults have developed around practitioners of scientific medicine whose patients came from lower socioeconomic levels. Moreno Cañas and Gregorio Hernández are part of the latter pattern. Both of their healing cults augment the adoration of healers by Catholics that is present in almost all Latin American societies (especially in popularized religion). A further pattern has fused non-Hispanic curative complexes with Hispanic healing traditions.[51]

Scholars debate the meanings of healing cults, but their potency is indisputable. Duncan Pedersen and Veronica Baruffati suggest that the cults represent "the incapacity of the state to satisfy growing social demands,"[52] and Setha Low describes Gregorio Hernández's cult as a "response of lay people to [the] medicalization of [health] care."[53] Michael Taussig relates that cults surrounding early scientific doctors, such as that of Gregorio Hernández, represent a response to modernity in which the "magic of science and industry . . . holds out the promise of the power and wealth of the modern world . . . denied [to] the vast majority of their patients."[54] The process of modernization, in particular secularization, appears to be closely associated with the emergence of healing cults. Although scholars might attribute their emergence to certain structural or social processes, it might also be that devotees simply seek relief through a medium that they think has the power of healing, one that is intimately linked to their religious beliefs.

Medical Pluralism

Imagine a young mother of three children living in Cali, Colombia. Like many people in her neighborhood, her mother lives with her, as does her aunt. She and her family suffer the normal episodes of ill health that afflict members of their community. When her son broke his leg playing soccer, she took him to the local clinic, where a professional doctor was able to set the bone successfully. She treated her daughter's fever with a poultice of onions applied to her feet. Shopping in the market, her mother regularly purchases the herbs that she uses to prepare teas to soothe her nerves, but the younger woman urges her to go to the homeopathic pharmacy a few blocks away, especially because one of its prescriptions did so well for her own headache. The aunt prays regularly to Gregorio Hernández to assist her with the cancer that doctors seem unable to treat, and the young mother has lit candles in the local church to seek his intercession and has spoken to the priest.

All these activities take place within a system of medical pluralism. They represent the sick person's casual usage of scientific, popular, and homeopathic medicines. They also indicate the persistence of humoral traits, as well as the primacy of Catholic healing beliefs within a household. Although the Colombian government has declared only scientific medicine to be official, social choices about where to seek relief are based on popular sensibilities about effective responses to different types of ailments, not on a government mandate.[55]

Medical pluralism emerged in Latin America over the past two centuries. A brief comparison of the medical systems of the northern Andes in the 1790s and in the present reveals the depth of the transformation. In the late eighteenth century, Hispanic medicine, which used humoral knowledge within a holistic Catholic frame of understanding, dominated the colonial medical spectrum. Most healing took place within an informal social setting, using either domestic medicine, empirics, or *curanderos*. Shamans healed in areas with significant numbers of indigenous peoples and also asserted an influence on Hispanic populations. A limited formal medical structure, incorporating institutions, titled healers, and legal authority, existed, but its weakness meant that most people had little, if any, contact with formal medicine. As a result, formal medicine had little social power. The Church, in both its institutional and its ideological dimensions, bridged the formal and informal spheres. In most instances, medical knowledge differed hardly at all in formal and informal settings because social and professional healers drew from the same corpus of knowledge.

Today a variety of medical systems operates within Colombia and Ecuador. Depending upon the locale, scientific medicine, homeopathy, popular medicine, spiritist healing, and indigenous systems are practiced. Generally speaking, urbanites have more options than rural dwellers, although class, ethnicity, and religion belie notions of medical choice. As it was two hundred years ago, domestic medicine is the initial response to healing, but the *materia medica* now includes the incredible pharmacopoeia associated with scientific medicine, as well as treatments from popular medicine. Scientific medicine, officially endorsed by the state, is sustained by a vast institutional presence including hospitals, schools, clinics, laboratories, pharmacies, professional associations, and a dense bureaucratic maze. It is supported by a corpus of laws and decrees that fully vest it with the authority and power of the state. Scientific medicine is fused with the state and also linked with a powerful international web of drug companies, medical associations, and suppliers of medical technology. Largely absent from official medicine is the Church, in either an institutional or an ideological sense. Scientific beliefs now dominate both formal and informal medicine, although humoral interpretations still influence the latter. Unlike their counterparts in the 1790s, the social and professional healers of the present day operate within fundamentally different worlds. Another difference is the presence of the cash nexus at the center of most medical systems, regardless of their ideology or methodology.[56]

How did this Great Transformation occur? An answer to that question is beyond the scope of this project, but a study of the conflicts that surrounded Miguel Perdomo Neira helps to establish the critical juncture of change. John Janzen notes that the organization of medical systems, which are synonymous with social systems, requires analysis by inquiries into their processes and changes. He asserts that "the effect of politics upon structural change in a social system is absolutely critical." Politics, he says, consists of the "exercise of power and authority,"[57] factors that were apparent in Perdomo's life. Janzen turns to Max Weber to identify three sources of authority: charismatic authority, which is vested in the character of a single person; authority that comes from a coherent set of beliefs and practices that are maintained by training and experience; and rational-legal authority, which originates in the laws, institutions, and bureaucracies of a state.[58] These processes dominated the period of Perdomo's life during the Great Transformation.

Scientific medicine was introduced into the northern Andes as an alien ideology representing the rational knowledge of Western Europe. Francisco Javier de Santa Cruz y Espejo, José Celestino Mutis, Padre Miguel de la Isla, and others introduced this knowledge into the formal system of medical education, most effectively in the 1802 plan of studies for the school of medicine in Bogotá, and it was then inculcated into a first generation of scientific doctors. The introduction of the French anatomoclinical method to Bogotá's Universidad Central prepared a second generation of doctors, including Antonio Vargas Reyes, who were, in turn, responsible for the institutionalization of scientific medicine in Colombia. Whereas scientific medicine had little authority in the 1790s, it had acquired significant potency by the 1870s from a now institutionalized set of beliefs, practices, and education. It was at that time that Perdomo sparked the confrontation between medical ideologies rooted in distinct sources of authority.

The institutionalization of scientific medicine in Ecuador was not accomplished until the early twentieth century, by which time scientific medicine in Colombia had acquired the rational-legal authority of the state. By the 1930s scientific medicine had become the official medicine throughout Latin America, assisted at every crucial step by political power. From its introduction in educational institutions, scientific medicine was slowly professionalized and authorized by the power of the state. It did not, however, completely eclipse other traditions, which continue to be practiced in changed and sometimes subordinated positions. Although scientific medicine dominates formal, legal, and institutional structures, earlier beliefs persist.

The colonial medical spectrum has been replaced by medical pluralism—one of the products of the Great Transformation. For healers caught up in the ideological contentions of the transformation, the struggles of the day were of fundamental importance. For most people, however, this change was not a traumatic process. Those in the popular level of society were very adaptable and saw few contradictions among the healers of distinct medical systems within a pluralist framework, even though they might have recognized the differing abilities of those healers in treating different maladies.[59] Carlos Viesca Treviño notes that "the officialization of scientific medicine" in the various social realities of Mexico was accompanied by the resignification and enrichment of traditional medicine.[60] Thus, our imagined resident of Cali has few difficulties in shifting from one medical system to another, however they might be perceived by the state or by medical practitioners.

Medical anthropologists (and others) differentiate between the concepts of disease and illness. Illnesses are the experiences suffered by a sick person, whereas diseases are the abnormalities in the function of the body as framed by a doctor. Disease, in this sense, originates in the mechanical representations of the body as portrayed by René Descartes, William Harvey, and countless other rationalists. The sick person becomes a patient whose diseased body is understood best by doctors.[61] Knowledge of illness and knowledge of disease might well be seen as analogous to the differences between social and professional medicine. Knowledge in social medicine is acquired experientially; knowledge in professional medicine is acquired through specialized institutional training. Vargas Reyes, in his belief in the anatomoclinical ideology, imagined the body to be a machine, and he felt that Perdomo's lack of knowledge in this area left him open to scientific critique. Scientific doctors, according to Gregory Pappas, acquire enormous power over a patient because of the disposition of the human body: "The patient becomes the docile body to be manipulated and explored, robbed of autonomy."[62] Yet despite this profound power of the body and the intimate knowledge of scientific healing, medical efficacy is often as much a product of the belief system of a culture as of a specific medical treatment.[63] The placebo effect, or the psychotherapeutic benefit, is undoubtedly greatest when the sick person and the doctor speak the same medical language— that is, in the practice of social medicine.

Perdomo would undoubtedly be classified as a social healer within a system of *medicina tradicional*. Vargas Reyes certainly was a professional healer and part of *medicina facultativa*. Perdomo had no formal training, worked within a familial network, and acquired his knowledge experientially. By contrast, Vargas Reyes was a consummate professional, with formal education, institutional affiliation, and membership in a professional association. For the person suffering from an illness in 1870s Bogotá, further distinctions could be made. Perdomo, *el médico del pueblo* (the people's doctor), spoke the same language as the sufferer, had the same understanding of illness, and shared the same moral code. Vargas Reyes and other practitioners of scientific medicine most likely framed diseases differently than did their patients, for their scientific medical knowledge did not correspond to the knowledge of Hispanic medicine. However, the sick person who sought the assistance of either Perdomo or Vargas Reyes was probably less interested in knowledge and more interested in curative relief. There is little evidence to suggest that the efficacy of either doctor was noticeably superior to that of the other. The testimonials often praised Perdomo because he cured patients when other doctors could not.

There surely were people who would have attested to the abilities of scientific doctors as well.

The most outstanding difference between Perdomo and professional doctors, as articulated in the testimonials, related to the healer's moral code—his attitude of Christian charity. Perdomo believed in a unified image of nature and God, one that saw God as the source of all cures. This ideology was shared by the ill people who sought his assistance, and it was deeply embedded within the Hispanic culture of the nineteenth century. The same belief system continues to sustain the healing cults of Gregorio Hernández and others. If, as Viesca Treviño suggests, traditional medicine survives in Mexico because it offers a holistic vision of the relationship between humans and the world about them,[64] then the intensity of the clash between Perdomo and professional doctors becomes more significant. This confrontation laid bare distinct notions of healing, ideology, and power in the northern Andes. Some of the divisions of contemporary Latin American society can be traced back to that moment in the Great Transformation. Folk medicine is valued, at least in part, because it is a component of a unified and more broadly accepted ideological framework in a way that scientific medicine is not. For many Latin Americans, the daily influence of faith and reason continues to be major social and intellectual realities.

Appendix

Testimonials on the Healings of Miguel Perdomo Neira

Document 1   *Un ultraje inmerecido* (Quito: Oficina Tipográfica de F. Bermeo, por J. Mora, 1867)

I, Father Manuel Valdez, a priest of the Convent of Nuestra Señora de Mercedes of this capital [Quito], certify before the law that upon hearing of the fame of the prodigious cures made by Mr. Miguel Perdomo I went to the canton of Otavalo . . . to be cured of the illness called *coto* that has afflicted me for many years and that has grown so severe as to almost stop my breathing. When Mr. Perdomo saw me, he undertook a cure with all the humanity and disinterest that characterizes him; he told me that this illness had caused me to lose my mind and that he was disposed to get rid of it forever, insofar as it had been cured two times already. He undertook a surgical operation of the throat with admirable dexterity and with the ability of a professor, and the success matched my expectations. I am now completely cured of the illness, and in the full use of my intellectual capacities that, as I had said earlier, I had lost on two occasions.

Quito
November 15, 1867
Father Manuel María Valdez

Mr. Miguel Perdomo
My very appreciated friend

Knowing that many certificates from persons whom you have cured will be published, please allow me the satisfaction of expressing

111

my acknowledgment of your prodigious cure of a grave illness of my left eye that had lasted for over a year, and assuring you that I am now safe and sound since the day that you performed the operation.

Gratitude obliges me to offer you my sincere thanks. Please consider me as your eternal friend.

Quito
November 22, 1867
Juan José Merizalde

◯ I swear upon my word of honor, from sentiments of gratitude, that as a consequence of a severe blow that I suffered in the year 1859, a cyst developed on the knee of my left leg, that continued to grow so that it impeded the flexibility and extension of the leg so that walking became quite difficult. In this situation, Mr. Miguel Perdomo Neira extracted the gland by way of a dexterous surgical operation, which allowed me to come to know his considerable talents. The wound is now closed; and in a matter of a few days I will be able to walk without difficulty.

Quito
September 28, 1867
J. Antonio Toledo

◯ In the legally approved style:—Salvador Huertas, citizen of Tulcan and visitor in this capital, appeared before a judge and said that over the space of forty-five years he had suffered from a cyst over his eyebrow, complicated by a chronic tumor on the same side of his forehead received in a fall from a horse some twenty years ago. He took the opportunity to present himself to Mr. Miguel Perdomo to seek his assistance. Perdomo, by his proven charity, made an incision, took a vial of green liquid mixed with some white particles, and from another bag took a portion of butter-like paste; as a result of these measures he is restored to health thanks to the help of that humane person. In addition he said that his son, Federico Huertas, also was cured of severe chills, with only five or six swallows of liquid from the aforesaid Perdomo, and remains in good health, and, by the legal code, attests to the truth of this statement.

Quito
October 16, 1867
Salvador Huertas
Rafael Venegas, political lieutenant

Father Joaquín López, of the preaching order of Our Father of Santo Domingo, certifies with complete truth and considering the merits of justice, that over the space of twenty years I have suffered an illness of the right leg, because of some contracted tendons, so that I could not walk well, which became so bad that I could not walk without the use of a cane: and it came to be worse and worse so that I had to spend much time in bed without hope of a cure so that I resolved to use two canes or else crutches to help me walk, when it occurred to me through the person of Mr. Miguel Perdomo Neira that the leg should be repaired, and out of diligence I went to Ibarra, where this knowledgeable person was, and by his applications and great honor he has left me free of that lesion, so that I don't have to use a cane and can walk freely through the streets thanks to God; I am convinced that I will remain completely healthy, altering the prescription over the next few months according to Mr. Perdomo; and because of this I offer the present testimony, and sign it in Quito, November 15, 1867.

Joaquín López
Nicanor Chiriboga, central judge

In the same manner Mr. Gabriel Jiménez attested and testified in a completely legal form, saying: that he did not have [ulterior] reasons for offering his deserved thanks to Mr. Miguel Perdomo in payment for having left him healthy and well from so critical and unfortunate a malady; because he had been left without any money, having spent it all over more than twenty years on so many doctors, and none of them had been able to significantly relieve the urinary ailment from which he had suffered. All their medicines had been no more than palliatives, while now he finds himself robust and healthy, and with the confidence that, thanks to God and the measures taken by Perdomo, he would not worsen again; and because of this, with great acknowledgments of gratitude, [he] offers the present document and signs it together with that of the certifying judge in Quito, November 15, 1867.

Gabriel Jiménez
Nicanor Chiriboga, central judge

The undersigned Asunción León, of this community, a single, adult woman, having to complete a justly held and deserved obligation, legally and solemnly swears before the true God who has to judge me, declares voluntarily and satisfactorily: that having spent a great amount of time of over 12 years with a cyst that protrudes from the corner of the left eye, not only [its] having impeded my vision, but having caused severe pain when it touched the nose, and making impossible many of the small, ordinary acts of domestic life; that in such a state, informed of this desperate and incurable condition by more that eight professors who refused to perform the operation I asked, but with the fortune that attends to the unfortunate, caused Mr. Miguel Perdomo to come to the city as an exceptional and mystical man to offer his infinite mercy to the city, and in less time than it took to offer this explanation, I was cured of that terrible illness, healthy and satisfied, and have remained well ever since, without any pain. The sight through my opened eye is better than ever, and I am unable to contain the satisfaction that I feel, not the least to the public for the fate of my soul, so I offer some sacrifice for the goodness that this celebrated man has brought to the city, with more retribution than persecution that is made before God and afflicted humanity.

Quito
November 7, 1867
Asunción León

Antonio Muñoz, the parochial judge of Chillogallo, certifies under the penalty of the law: that having suffered over the course of more than six years a grave and painful illness complicated by pneumonia, liver irritation, violent stomach pains, all that made me suffer indescribable pains, that forced me to go to various [medical] faculties of the capital to seek their cure, and in effect finding that none of their prescriptions resulted in any improvement, and finding myself prostrate in bed, ill disposed of even surviving, knowing that Mr. Miguel Perdomo had come to the city, asked him a favor, that he generous and honorably granted; [he] came to visit me in the parish, and finding me prostrate with pain and fearful for my life, after a tedious examination and by making me answer many questions, said that you have a severe complication of the aforementioned problems, and in addition you have a problem with your interior veins; and, despite this, he offered to cure me and make me healthy, and as a result after ten days of giving me applications, he made me healthy and cured, so that after fifteen days I could ride a horse and carry out all of the other functions that my job requires, leaving me well and healthy, thanks to the aforementioned Mr. Perdomo; and in obligation for the eternal gratitude that I profess in my heart for my honorable benefactor, confirmed this statement in the parish of Santiago of Chillogallo.

November 8, 1867
Antonio Muñoz, parochial judge

The undersigned, completing an obligation of justice and with sentiments of gratitude, under the legal penalty of sworn testimony, declares: that my wife, Mrs. Teresa Bravo, was seized by a life-threatening illness, [so I] took her to be cared for by a series of respected [physicians]; the professors knew that the problem was a *saratan* that she had on her back but they declared themselves incapable of removing it because it would be a dangerous and difficult operation. After a period of eight years, it became necessary to do something and when the presence of Mr. Miguel Perdomo in the city was announced, a man who was making prodigious cures, especially in the area of surgery, I convinced him to come to the parish of Machachi, the place of my residence, and I presented her to him at the earliest occasion; he proceeded to examine her and announced that given the nature and character of her illness, he removed the *saratan* in less time than it took him to say it, and closed the skin that he opened for the operation, and at the end of eleven days she was completely well and barely showed the scar of the operation. After one month she remains well and cured of the illness and has had no recurrence, which is but an eternal reminder of his prodigious cures. I testify in justice and in recognition.

Quito
November 18, 1872
Vicente Rafael Teran

CℋO In the same way there appeared Mr. José Hurtado, a citizen of the capital and in the legally prescribed manner said: that having extreme gratitude to Mr. Miguel Perdomo Neira who does me the honor of accepting this certificate in payment for the favor done by Mr. Perdomo in restoring my health, curing me of a powerful nervous attack that required that I remain bedridden without moving, suffering a horrible pain in my legs with the slightest movement, so that I could not get out of bed without crying out; in this state I resolved to call upon a professor of the city and a well-known and able empiric, and neither one nor the other was able to help me at all, but to the contrary left me in worse pain; and so a few days later [I] made the effort, on crutches, to seek the protection of Mr. Perdomo, who examined me and applied six ointments that he rubbed together, and I am now walking healthily and without crutches on my own feet; and in order to pay back Mr. Perdomo with honor, the undersigned presents these documents before a judge who certifies them.

Quito
November 2, 1867
The mark of the witness
Santiago Herrería, parochial lieutenant

CℋO Baldomira Estupiñan, also a resident of the capital, in the same manner as the earlier testimony appeared and said: that she un-

expectedly was forced into bed with a violent stomach pain complicated by a shoulder pain that stretched into her body, that from the
circumstance of the illness she knew that she was going to die; as a
result [she] went to her confessor and the medical facilities of the
country; they tried to alleviate her pain but it was impossible to help
her or to offer her confession. Upon the request of the moribund
woman Mr. Miguel Perdomo Neira appeared to offer her assistance,
who ordered her to take some medicine at ten o'clock at night in the
presence of her mother, Mrs. Ramona Estupiñan; afterwards she began to improve, speaking and offering thanks to God. The people
around her were alarmed and responded that *this is a miraculous resur-
rection.* The following day Perdomo ordered another dose, which she
took, and the patient declared that day that she was as healthy as
before, and in payment offers this statement of appreciation before
the justice and signed the testimony with the judge of Quito this first
day of November 1867. Another thing. She states that the medical
facility that she had visited was the best in the country and that they
had prescribed bleeding and took eighteen ounces of blood as the
only way to save her life; the patient did not show any improvement
until she took the doses from Perdomo, who deserved the corresponding gratitude. There follows the rubric of the woman who does not
know how to read or write and that of the judge.

Manuel Soberon
Santiago Herrería, parochial lieutenant

In the same way Mr. Fidel de la Guerra, resident of the capital, appeared and testified: that with sentiments of gratitude and justice, [he] declares that within two days of taking two doses of medicine
[from Miguel Perdomo Neira], has had his sight completely restored
from an injury that had happened four years ago, signed before the
certifying judge.

Quito

November 4, 1867
Fidel de la Guerra
Rafael Venegas, political lieutenant

DOCUMENT 2   *La Ilustración*, April 9, 1872

DECLARATION OF GRATITUDE

Dr. Miguel Perdomo Neira

Please allow me to declare my gratitude for the great benefit that you have done me to cure me and leave me healthy and well; and for the public's knowledge allow me to offer the following account.

For more than fourteen years I have suffered a troubling urinary illness that has left me cruelly tormented, reaching the point where at times I could not urinate. Over the years many physicians have examined me, to whom I've paid the money that they asked, without regaining my health, or without their repaying me. When the news of the surprising cures of Dr. Miguel Perdomo Neira came to my attention, and finding myself completely worse, I arranged to be taken to San Juan de Rioseco, where [Perdomo] was, and presented myself to him so that he could explain the illness that I had.

After seeing me, he said: you have gallstones, and this is the reason why you can't urinate and are afflicted with such pains. It is necessary to remove the stones. Four days later he performed the operation and removed three stones: one the size of a grain of cacao, and the other two a little smaller. This operation was done in the presence of the Alcalde and of his Secretary Félix Santos and in the presence of Mr. Nicolás Pontón and of Dr. Antonio José Gutiérrez, the priest of this district; all of whom collected the stones after their removal.

I declare, then, that I am now well and cured of that illness that had afflicted me and am left in complete tranquillity. I pray that God repays Mr. Perdomo for all the charitable acts that he has done for humanity and that he be free of the jealous shots aimed at him.

Guaduas
March 2, 1872
Ignacio Vera

DOCUMENT 3   *La Ilustración*, May 2, 1872

Crisóstomo Rico, Judge of the district of Ambalema in the Sovereign State of Tolima, certified: that I personally know Mr. Aguedo

Lináres, a native and citizen of this district, who came before me to declare. I received him in the legal manner, and after reading to him the legal penalties of giving false testimony, [he] expounded: "That since a little more than ten years of age there appeared and continued to develop a cancerous tumor under the right eye, one that filled the bony cavity and expanded from there, it later grew so that it displaced the eye an inch from its normal cavity and damaged its vision: that having consulted with able doctors about this infirmity, they declared that they could not perform the extraction because of the difficulties [that the operation] would entail; [and] that to perform the operation it would require the removal of the afflicted organ, and others assured me that the operation would endanger my life; and that, guided by the fame that precedes, accompanies, and follows Dr. Miguel Perdomo Neira, the declarant went to look for him in Lérida in order to seek a consultation; that the doctor received him with goodness and revived his bitter hopes; that last December 4, in the presence of Pastor Lezama Armero, of Dr. Arístedes Terreros and of other respectable people, Dr. Perdomo, who was found bathing in the Bledo river, along with the testifier; the able surgeon, with only a common razor, removed the tumor, which was the size of a hen's egg, with small, painless incisions, and then with constant applications, the eye returned to almost its original position, and much of its sight of earlier years was restored. That in this manner the witness declares as a homage to the ability and surgical skill of Dr. Perdomo, asserting that the charity of this man is not inferior to that of science, insofar as in this declaration, nor in the declarations of thousands of poor people whom he has cured, has [Perdomo] charged for his assistance, nor for his medical prescriptions, as the inhabitants of Lérida, Ambalema, and thousands of other places can attest." This is what the aforementioned Mr. Aguedo Lináres said before the below-inscribed Judge and his Secretary. The testament was read to the witness, who affirms and ratifies under the force of law that it is true; and it was signed by the declarant with that of the Judge and Secretary in Ambalema, the 17th of January, 1872.

Aguedo Lináres
Crisóstomo Rico, judge
Gumersindo Saldúa, secretary

DOCUMENT 4   *La Ilustración*, May 7, 1872

PRODIGIOUS CURES

Before the judge who certifies this document, Mrs. Luisa Tovar presents, on pain of the legal penalties against false testimony and perjury, the testimony that I legally recorded before the penalty of the law: that because of a fever that she had for forty days, she remained crippled for five months, requiring the support of a cane or of two people to move about the house or from one place to another; and that now she finds her health restored thanks to the medical applications of Dr. Miguel Perdomo Neira over the course of six days, allowing the exponent to walk from her house to the church without any help, even though the surface is poorly paved and is six or seven blocks away.

That she also declares that for this cure Dr. Perdomo Neira did not ask for even one centavo nor any for the medications.

That in homage to his careful attention, to his goodness, and to his dedication to excessive charity, not only to the witness, but also to the thousands of people on whom he has performed such acts, she affirms and ratifies, speaking that she is a citizen of this district and is fifty years old. And the testimony is signed by the inscribed Judge and Secretary in Ambalema, the 18th of January, 1872.

Luisa Tovar
Crisóstomo Rico, judge
Gumersindo Saldúa, secretary

DOCUMENT 5   *La Ilustración*, May 8, 1872

PRODIGIOUS CURES

Monday, the sixth of this month we were present in the house of Dr. Miguel Perdomo Neira, [while] he operated on Toribia Castro, to extract a tumor that he had upon his shoulder. There was neither hemorrhage nor pain. The incident which we report was witnessed by over fifty people.

Bogotá
May 7, 1872
M. A. Delgado
Enrique Umaúa Jimeno

⟨ℱ⟩ From Martin Ramírez, 25 years old, he extracted in my presence and with countless others, a tumor over the left eye, which had been there since birth.

Bogotá
May 7, 1872
Enrique Umaúa Jimeno

⟨ℱ⟩ From Mrs. Victoria de San José, he extracted, in the presence of the Reverend Father Francisco Ospina and Mrs. Virginia Silva, Mercédes Defrancisco, and Mercédes Sandino, a tumor that she had on her left arm for more than twenty years. This operation was performed without blood or pain.

Bogotá
May 7, 1872
Saturnino Vergara

⟨ℱ⟩ Before the certifying Judge, Mr. José María Devia, who has been legally recorded, according to all requirements of the law, and under which he said: he has suffered a grave infirmity in his right eye since his birth that has caused him extreme and immense pain; and that for all of these forty years, no one has been able to restore his health, in spite of visits to various doctors, until he presented himself to Dr. Miguel Perdomo Neira, who in the first moment that he saw him, offered to cure him; that [Perdomo] fulfilled this, and on this date he finds himself healthy and well, thanks to the grace of Providence; he explained the symptoms of the illness: he had a tumor on the right eye that protruded out of the socket, so that he could not see the pupil because of that cancer, which caused him excruciating pains;

That he suffered from rheumatism that hampered his work, and that now he is healthy and well because all of his illnesses have disappeared thanks to the medications and surgeries of Dr. Miguel Perdomo Neira, who asked not even one centavo for his cures.

This is the truth, as said before the witnesses, and reread to the witness, who affirmed and attested to it, stating that he is a citizen of this district and forty years old, and that, since he could not sign his name, [it] is signed by a witness in his name, with me the certifying judge, in Ambalema, January 18, 1872.

The mark of José María Devia
Crisóstomo Rico, judge
Fulgencio Cardoso
Gumersindo Saldúa, secretary

DOCUMENT 6   *La Ilustración*, May 21, 1872

JUSTICE AND RECOGNITION

Dr. Miguel Perdomo N. has had to leave Bogotá because the hatred and envy [there] has not been stilled; this privileged man, who is absolutely dedicated to the alleviation of those who suffer agonies because of their illnesses, has been seen as a benefactor of those in agony. Nothing has been able to contain those who, interested in denigrating this man, [who,] suffering the discomforts of a long journey, came to this city to look for those who suffer in order to alleviate their illnesses; to help the needy and afflicted in order to console them.

What have the enemies of Perdomo accomplished? They have shown themselves to be dominated by hatred; they have brought to light the merits of this upright and humanitarian man, and aligned the suffering public on the side of his compassionate good deeds.

But when hatred and bad manners speak, those who have received the benefits of this well-meaning healer ought not to remain quiet. Justice and gratitude demand that we speak, and because of this I am going to offer a testimony to the cure he effected on my young daughter.

Allow me to make a few brief references to the incident.

I had consulted with various doctors about what had caused the constant pain in the bladder of my daughter, a girl of three years old; all of them told me that the cause was a bladder irritation, and that in order to get rid of it several prescriptions were required, but they were all in vain; the girl continued in the same condition, until I spoke with Dr. Perdomo, on the fourth of this month, when he examined her and offered to cure her, saying that she had a bladder stone and that she would not need an operation to be healed. He gave her a single dose of powder and three days later, after she passed the stone, she remained in perfect health.

The stone was two centimeters long and can be seen in this print-shop, so that those who want to see it can [do so].

Praise to Mr. Perdomo, destined by Providence to alleviate the suffering of the poor. I hope that he receives the [most] profound recognition for the good that he has done in bringing my young innocent girl back to health. God will compensate him for this enormous good deed that he has done. I can only offer him my gratitude and acknowledgment; and day after day I will teach my daughter to venerate the prodigious man who has done this much-appreciated service to her health.

Bogotá
May 19, 1872
Fermín Rivas Rodríguez

DOCUMENT 7   *La Ilustración*, May 28, 1872

STATEMENT OF GRATITUDE

Dr. Miguel Perdomo N.—Bogotá

The undersigned residents of the district of Serrezuela, desiring to manifest our profound recognition for all the services that you have given to afflicted people during your short stay in this place, have the honor of directing to you this statement seeking your friendship, as a proof of our eternal gratitude.

Nothing can compensate you for your care and attention; for the correctness, liberality, and dedication that you employed in the

alleviation of the affronts that those who implore your acknowledgments as a surgeon and doctor suffered; we cannot repay you with
money, so that this is a small notice of our sentiments for you and
your ardent charity; but there exists in our hearts, a very uncommon
sentiment, the recognition of your merits that our gratitude will always keep with us: honor us by accepting this statement, sir, and take
into account the knowledge that in Serrezuela you have admirers of
your virtues; and that in whatever situation, in whatever circumstance,
we will receive you with open arms, and that we will bless the day
when you return to the land where you are so loved and venerated.

Accept, then, sir, these sentiments of distinguished respect with
which we have the honor to implore you, from your loyal servants.

[There follows 54 signatures.]
Serrezuela, May 5, 1872

DOCUMENT 8   *La Ilustración*, June 11, 1872

Mr. Luciano Lerchundi voluntarily presented himself in the office of the alcalde of the district of Lérida on the 20th of December
past, asking that he might receive the following legal declaration, and
this alcalde, in accordance with the legal formalities, received this statement: "That for more than thirty years he had suffered from clouded
sight, which had led him to seek the counsel of the best doctors, Julian
Jérviz, Antonio Mendoza and others: that over time they made various applications that had not improved things in the least; that today
he finds himself completely recovered thanks to Dr. Miguel Perdomo
Neira, who over thirty-four days took on the responsibility to cure
him, which he has [done] under the treatment that he recommended."

The declarant also said that he could not see well enough to read
or write without glasses and that now he has full sight without the
need for them.

The declarant also said that Dr. Perdomo applied his medicines
without asking any fee and made no distinction between rich and
poor.

He declared also that he [Perdomo] was available for public service at all hours of the day or night and saw more than two thousand persons who sought his acts of charity.

All that he declared is attested to be the truth before the law, and having read his resolution, he signed and ratified it, stating that he was an adult of fifty years, signing this certificate before the alcalde and secretary.

Luciano Lerchundi
Antonio Terreros, alcalde
Antonio Zúñiga, secretary

Notes

Introduction, Pages xi–xix

1. *El Tradicionista*, May 7, 1872.
2. *La Ilustración*, April 9, 1872.
3. Ibid., May 28, 1872.
4. Ibid., April 9, 1872.
5. *El Diario de Cundinamarca*, May 7, 1872.
6. Ibid., May 13, 1872. Italics added.
7. For examples, see Mauro Madero Moreira, *Historia de la medicina en la provincia del Guayas* (Guayaquil, Ecuador, 1955), and Pedro María Ibáñez, *Memorias para la historia de la medicina en Santafé de Bogotá* (Bogotá, 1968).
8. Medical systems are conceptual entities that encompass the beliefs and knowledge of illness, the techniques and tools associated with healing, and the institutions and social structures that sustain healing.
9. John M. Janzen, "The Comparative Study of Medical Systems as Changing Social Systems," *Social Science and Medicine* 12:2B (1978), 122.
10. Byron J. Good, *Medicine, Rationality, and Experience: An Anthropological Perspective* (New York, 1994), 167.
11. The literature on medical pluralism is quite rich, though the term itself is used differently by many scholars. For an introduction to the topic, see Arthur Kleinman, "Concepts and a Model for the Comparison of Medical Systems as Cultural Systems," *Social Science and Medicine* 12 (1978), 85–95, and Duncan Pedersen and Veronica Baruffati, "Healers, Deities, Saints and Doctors: Elements for the Analysis of Medical Systems," *Social Science and Medicine* 29:4 (1989), 487–96.
12. Pedersen and Baruffati, "Healers, Deities, Saints and Doctors," 487.

Chapter 1, Pages 1–31

1. *La Ilustración*, May 14, 1872. I am grateful to Professor Henry Thurston-Griswold for his translation.
2. *La Ilustración*, May 8, 1872.

3. Kleinman, "Concepts and a Model for the Comparison of Medical Systems as Cultural Systems," 87, 88.

4. Good, *Medicine, Rationality, and Experience*, 53. See also Leon Eisenberg, "Disease and Illness: Distinctions between Professional and Popular Ideas of Sickness," *Culture, Medicine and Psychiatry* 1:1 (1977), 11.

5. Charles Rosenberg, "Introduction: Framing Disease—Illness, Society, and History," in *Framing Disease: Studies in Cultural History*, ed. by Charles E. Rosenberg and Janet Golden (New Brunswick, NJ, 1992).

6. Irwin Press, "Problems in the Definition and Classification of Medical Systems," *Social Science and Medicine* 1:14B (1980), 47.

7. Pedersen and Baruffati, "Healers, Deities, Saints and Doctors," 487.

8. Ibid., 489.

9. Rosenberg, "Introduction: Framing Disease," xvii.

10. Virginia Gutiérrez de Pineda, *Medicina tradicional de Colombia: Magía, religión y curanderismo*, 2 vols. (Bogotá, 1985), 1:71–74.

11. Laurel Thatcher Ulrich, *A Midwife's Tale: The Life of Martha Ballard, Based on Her Diary, 1785–1812* (New York, 1990), 61–62; Gutiérrez de Pineda, *Medicina tradicional*, 2:27.

12. Robert T. Trotter II and Juan Antonio Chavira, *Curanderismo: Mexican American Folk Healing* (Athens, GA, 1981), 1–2.

13. Ibid., 2.

14. Françoise Loux, "Folk Medicine," in *Companion Encyclopedia of the History of Medicine*, ed. by W. F. Bynum and Roy Porter, 2 vols. (New York, 1993), 1:665.

15. Daniel E. Moerman, "Physiology and Symbols: The Anthropological Implications of the Placebo Effect," in *The Anthropology of Medicine: From Culture to Method*, ed. by Lola Romanucci-Ross, Daniel E. Moerman, and Laurence R. Tancredi, 2nd ed. (New York, 1991), 130–31.

16. Isaac F. Holton, *New Granada: Twenty Months in the Andes* (New York, 1857), 233.

17. Friedrich Hassaurek, *Four Years among Spanish Americans* (London, 1868), 202–6.

18. Pedersen and Baruffati, "Healers, Saints, Dieties and Doctors," 489.

19. *La Ilustración*, June 4, 1872.

20. Peter Wright and Andrew Treacher, *The Problem of Medical Knowledge: Examining the Social Construction of Medicine* (Edinburgh, 1982), 6.

21. *El Tradicionista*, May 14, 1872.

22. Trotter and Chavira, *Curanderismo*, 18–23.

23. Libbet Crandon-Malamud, *From the Fat of Our Souls: Social Change, Political Process, and Medical Pluralism in Bolivia* (Berkeley, CA, 1991).

24. Suzanne Austin Alchon, *Native Society and Disease in Colonial Ecuador* (New York, 1991), 7; David Bushnell, *The Making of Modern Colombia: A Nation in Spite of Itself* (Berkeley, CA, 1993), 3–7.

25. Andrés Soriano Lleras, *La medicina en el Nuevo Reino de Granada, durante la conquista y la colonia* (Bogotá, 1972), 3–66.

26. Eduardo Estrella, *Medicina aborigen: La práctica médica aborigen de la sierra ecuatoriana* (Quito, 1978), 217–18. See also Mircea Eliade, *Shamanism: Archaic Techniques of Ecstasy*, trans. by Willard R. Trask (Princeton, NJ, 1972), 288–336, passim.

27. Silvio Luis Haro Alvear, *Shamanismo en el Reino de Quito* (Quito, 1973), 12–21.

28. Soriano Lleras, *La medicina en la colonia*, 17–24.

29. Frank Salomon, "The Fury of Andrés Arévalo: Disease Bundles of a Colonial Andean Shaman," in *Political Anthropology of Ecuador*, ed. by Jeffrey Ehrenrich (Albany, NY, 1985), 83–105.

30. Joseph William Bastien, *Healers of the Andes: Kallawaya Herbalists and Their Medicinal Plants* (Salt Lake City, UT, 1987), 34.

31. Ibid.

32. Ibid., 34, 35.

33. Bastien refers to Kallawaya medicine as a "holistically oriented, traditional system . . . that cares for spiritual, environmental, and social aspects of sick persons as well as their physical ailments (a concern with the total meaning of illness)"; see ibid., 11.

34. Soriano Lleras, *La medicina en la colonia*, 14–17.

35. Estrella, *Medicina aborigen*, 218–20; Bastien, *Healers of the Andes*, 16, 46; Alchon, *Native Society and Disease*, 26–31.

36. "Many of these sorcerers are *ambicamayos*, as they call themselves, or healers, but they precede their cures with superstitious and idolatrous practices." See Pablo Joseph de Arriaga, *The Extirpation of Idolatry in Peru*, trans. and ed. by L. Clark Keating (Lexington, KY, 1968), 99. See, for example, Irene Silverblatt, "The Evolution of Witchcraft and the Meaning of Healing in Colonial Andean Society," *Culture, Medicine, and Psychiatry* 7 (1983), 413–27, or Bonnie Glass-Coffin, *The Gift of Life: Female Spirituality and Healing in Northern Peru* (Albuquerque, NM, 1999), 37–46.

37. Carlos Viesca Treviño, "La medicina tradicional mexicana," in *Memorias del simposio medicina tradicional, curanderismo y cultura popular en Colombia de hoy: Curanderismo, parte 1°*, by the Instituto Colombiano de Antropología (Bogotá, 1990), 16–18.

38. Michael Taussig, *Shamanism, Colonialism, and the Wild Man: A Study in Terror and Healing* (Chicago, 1987), passim.

39. David C. Lindberg, *The Beginnings of Western Science: The European Scientific Tradition in Philosophical, Religious, and Institutional Context, 600 B.C. to A.D. 1450* (Chicago, 1992), 113–16.

40. George M. Foster, "On the Origin of Humoral Medicine in Latin America," *Medical Anthropology Quarterly* 1:4 (December 1987), 359; Vivian Nutton,

"Humoralism," in *Companion Encyclopedia of the History of Medicine*, ed. by W. F. Bynum and Roy Porter, 2 vols. (New York, 1993), 1:281–82.

41. Good, *Medicine, Rationality, and Experience*, 103–8.

42. Foster, "Humoral Medicine in Latin America," 359; Lindberg, *Western Science*, 116–17.

43. Good, *Medicine, Rationality, and Experience*, 112–13.

44. Lindberg, *Western Science*, 126.

45. Ibid., 170.

46. Ibid., 318–20. On p. 323, however, Lindberg notes that "only two or three of Galen's works were available in Latin before the eleventh century, whereas Hunayn ibn Ishaq (808–73) listed 129 Galenic works known to him in Baghdad."

47. Ibid., 204–6.

48. Ibid., 332–35.

49. Marie-Christine Pouchelle, *The Body and Surgery in the Middle Ages*, trans. by Rosemary Morris (Cambridge, 1990), 16–17, 20; Ghislaine Lawrence, "Surgery (Traditional)," in *Companion Encyclopedia of the History of Medicine*, ed. by W. F. Bynum and Roy Porter, 2 vols. (New York, 1993), 2:968–72.

50. *La Ilustración*, April 9, 1872.

51. *Enciclopedia de la religión católica*, 7 vols. (Barcelona, 1951), 2:450–53.

52. Christ is reputed to have cured on at least thirty-five occasions and is often depicted as a healer. See, for example, Sjaak Van der Geest, "Christ as Pharmacist: Medical Symbols in German Devotion," *Social Science and Medicine* 39:5 (1994), 727–32, and Roy Porter, "Religion and Medicine," in *Companion Encyclopedia of the History of Medicine*, ed. by W. F. Bynum and Roy Porter, 2 vols. (New York, 1993), 2:1452.

53. Owsei Temkin, *Hippocrates in a World of Pagans and Christians* (Baltimore, MD, 1991), 144, 160, 162.

54. Nancy G. Siraisi, *Medieval and Early Renaissance Medicine: An Introduction to Knowledge and Practice* (Chicago, 1990), 8, 11, 26–43.

55. Atwood D. Gaines and Paul E. Farmer, "Visible Saints: Social Cynosures and Dysphoria in the Mediterranean Tradition," *Culture, Medicine, and Psychiatry* 10 (1986), 298.

56. Donald Weinstein and Rudolph M. Bell, *Saints and Society: The Two Worlds of Western Civilization, 1000–1700* (Chicago, 1982), 135–36, 143–44, 157–58, 160.

57. Peter Brown, *The Cult of the Saints: Its Rise and Function in Latin Christianity* (Chicago, 1981), 114–20.

58. Gaines and Farmer, "Visible Saints," 299–300.

59. *La Ilustración*, June 4, 1872.

60. José María Cordovez Moure, *Reminiscencias—Santa Fé y Bogotá*, 9 vols., 6th ed. (Bogotá, 1942), 7:350, 353.

61. Anthony Luttrell, "The Earliest Hospitallers," in *Montjoie: Studies in Crusade History in Honour of Hans Eberhard Mayer*, ed. by Benjamin Z. Kedar, Jonathan Riley-Smith, and Rudolf Hiestand (Aldershot, England, 1997), 37–54.

62. C. H. Lawrence, *Medieval Monasticism: Forms of Religious Life in Western Europe in the Middle Ages*, 2nd ed. (New York, 1989), 211–14.

63. *Diccionario de historia eclesiástica de España*, 4 vols. (Madrid, 1972), 2:1248–49; M. Zuñiga Cisneros, "España, la medicina religiosa y los hospitales," *Archivo iberoamericano de historia de la medicina y antropología médica* 8 (1956), 385; Grace Golden, "Juan de Dios and the Hospital of Christian Charity," *Journal of the History of Medicine and Allied Sciences* 33 (1978), 60–34; Ruben D. Rumbaut, *John of God: His Place in the History of Psychiatry and Medicine* (Miami, FL, 1978), 23–29.

64. Sebastián Monteserrat Figueras, *Las actividades médico-castrenses de la inclita orden hospitalaria de San Juan de Dios* (Madrid, 1950), 73–76.

65. Ibid.

66. Patricia Vila de Pineda, "Algunos aspectos del estudio de la medicina tradicional en Colombia," in *Memorias del simposio medicina tradicional, curanderismo y cultura popular en Colombia de hoy: Curanderismo, parte 1°*, by the Instituto Colombiano de Antropología (Bogotá, 1990), 27.

67. This interpretation borrows heavily from Emilio Quevedo V., *Historia social de la ciencia en Colombia: Medicina (1)—Institucionalización de la medicina en Colombia, 1492–1860, Antecedentes de un proceso*, 9 vols. (Bogotá, 1993), 7:37–42.

68. John Tate Lanning, *The Royal Protomedicato: The Regulation of the Medical Professions in the Spanish Empire*, ed. by John Jay TePaske (Durham, NC, 1985), 17.

69. Quevedo V., *Institucionalización de la medicina*, 47–48.

70. Enrique Perdiguero, "Protomedicato y curanderismo," *Dynamis* 16 (1996), 91–108.

71. Francisco Guerra, "The Role of Religion in Spanish American Medicine," in *Medicine and Culture*, ed. by F. N. L. Poynter (London, 1969), 424, 427.

72. Idem, "Medical Education in Iberoamerica," in *The History of Medical Education*, ed. by C. D. O'Malley (Berkeley, CA, 1970), 419–21.

73. Ibid., 427, 429–31.

74. Agustín Albarracín Tevlón, "La medicina española de los siglos XVI, XVII, y XVIII y su influencia en Colombia," *Cuadernos Hispanoamericanos* 472 (October 1989), 40.

75. Guenter Risse, "Medicine in New Spain," in *Medicine in the New World: New Spain, New France, and New England*, ed. by Ronald L. Numbers (Knoxville, TN, 1987), 13–14.

76. Mark A. Burkholder and Lyman L. Johnson, *Colonial Latin America*, 2nd ed. (New York, 1994), 215.

77. Risse, "Medicine in New Spain," 14.

78. Lanning, *Royal Protomedicato*, passim; Risse, "Medicine in New Spain," 29–33.

79. Foster, "Humoral Medicine in Latin America," 363.

80. Risse, "Medicine in New Spain," 33–37. Galenic texts survived until 1838 in Chile. See Foster, "Humoral Medicine in Latin America," 363.

81. Guerra, "Religion in Spanish American Medicine," 180.

82. Risse, "Medicine in New Spain," 37–42.

83. Foster, "Humoral Medicine in Latin America," 363–65.

84. Lanning, *Royal Protomedicato*, 42.

85. Risse, "Medicine in New Spain," 46–51.

86. Foster, "Humoral Medicine in Latin America," 365–67.

87. Alchon, *Native Society and Disease*, 72.

88. Ibid., 72–76.

89. Shaman, *Medicina y economía: Un estudio de la evolución histórica de la relación entre medicina y estructura socioeconómica en el Ecuador* (Quito, 1979), 127–28.

90. Risse, "Medicine in New Spain," 33.

91. Ibid., 31–33.

92. Noemí Quezada, "The Inquisition's Repression of *Curanderos*," in *Cultural Encounters: The Impact of the Inquisition in Spain and the New World*, ed. by Mary Elizabeth Perry and Anne J. Cruz (Berkeley, CA, 1991), 37–57.

93. Soriano Lleras, *La medicina en la colonia*, 287.

94. Lanning, *Royal Protomedicato*, 138.

95. Ibid., 152, passim; idem, "The Illicit Practice of Medicine in the Spanish Empire in America," in *Homenaje a Don José María de la Peña Camara* (Madrid, 1969), 143–79. See also Gerardo Paz Otero, "Medicina colonial en Popayán," *Boletín Cultural y Bibliográfico* 10:3 (March 1967), 517.

96. Ibáñez, *Memorias*, 14–17; idem, *Crónicas de Bogotá*, 4 vols. (Bogotá, 1951), 1:71, 175; Quevedo V., *Institucionalización de la medicina*, 54–58.

97. Soriano Lleras, *La medicina en la colonia*, 73–76.

98. Juan Rodríguez Freyle, *El carnero*, ed. by Dario Achury Valenzuela (Caracas, 1979), 234.

99. Soriano Lleras, *La medicina en la colonia*, 107; idem, *Crónica del hospital de San Juan de Dios desde su fundación hasta su administración por la Junta de Beneficencia de Cundinamarca, 1654–1869* (Bogotá, 1964), 9–11.

100. Ibáñez, *Memorias*, 13–15; Salvador Clavijo y Clavijo, *La obra de la orden hospitalaria de San Juan de Dios en América y Filipinas* (Madrid, 1950), 75–76; Guerra, "Medical Education," 443–44; Soriano Lleras, *La medicina en la colonia*, passim.

101. Quevedo V., *Institucionalización de la medicina*, 119.

102. Soriano Lleras, *La medicina en la colonia*, 74.

103. Ibáñez, *Memorias*, 12.

104. Ibid., 14–15.

105. Soriano Lleras, *La medicina en la colonia*, 129–33.

106. Gualberto Arcos, *Evolución de la medicina en el Ecuador*, 3rd ed. (Quito, 1979), 231; Shaman, *Medicina y economía*, 127.

107. Nicolás Larco Noboa, Juanita Rebeca Larco Noboa, Santiago F. Larco Noboa, and Patricio Jarrín Molina, *Historia de la medicina ecuatoriana* (Quito, 1990), 54.

108. Arcos, *Evolución de la medicina*, 197, 201, 231.

109. Alchon, *Native Society and Disease*, 43–46.

110. Arcos, *Evolución de la medicina*, 205, 241.

111. Alchon, *Native Society and Disease*, 44.

112. Arcos, *Evolución de la medicina*, 147–50, 202–5.

113. Alchon, *Native Society and Disease*, 66–72.

114. Ibid., 70–71.

115. For a survey of healers in Mexico in that era, see Luz María Hernández Sáenz, *Learning to Heal: The Medical Profession in Colonial Mexico, 1767–1831* (New York, 1997).

116. Arcos, *Evolución de la medicina*, 192; Humberto Rosselli, "Relación de médicos y notables empíricos," *Médicos* 3 (1979), 59.

117. Eduardo Hidalgo Gamarra, "Desenvolvimiento de la medicina en el Ecuador," in *Primer Congreso Médico Ecuatoriano: Actas y trabajos* (Guayaquil, 1916), 193.

118. Ibáñez, *Crónicas de Bogotá*, 123–24.

119. Ibid., 124.

120. Larco Noboa et al., *Historia de la medicina ecuatoriana*, 27; Arcos, *Evolución de la medicina*, 193.

121. For the later view see George M. Foster, *Hippocrates' Latin American Legacy: Humoral Medicine in the New World* (Langhorne, PA, 1994). Barbara Tedlock (and others) dispute Foster's "diffusionist" theory, contending that hot-cold dichotomies are nearly universal and that anthropologists should look to the syncretism of medical systems and, more significantly, to the "the exploration of meaning" of healing and medicine within cultural systems. See Tedlock, "An Interpretive Solution to the Problem of Humoral Medicine in Latin America," *Social Science and Medicine* 24:12 (1987), 1069–71. See also Joseph William Bastien, "Differences between Kallawaya-Andean and Greek-European Humoral Theory," *Social Science and Medicine* 28:1 (1989), 45–51.

122. Rodríguez Freyle, *El carnero*, 288.

123. Hassaurek, *Four Years among Spanish Americans*, 113.

124. Manuel Uribe Angel, *La medicina en Antioquia* (Bogotá, 1936), 24. See also Holton, *Twenty Months in the Andes*, 146, 233, 384.

125. Ibáñez, *Memorias*, 26, 29–34; idem, *Crónicas de Bogotá*, 2:121–23.

126. Uribe Angel, *La medicina en Antioquia*, 14, 38.

127. Ibid., 14.

Chapter 2, Pages 33–59

1. Medardo Rivas, "Perdomo," *Obras de Medardo Rivas: Parte primera* (Bogotá, 1883), 223–27.

2. J. N. Hays, *The Burdens of Disease: Epidemics and Human Response in Western History* (New Brunswick, NJ, 1998), 89–90.

3. Roger French, "Sickness and the Soul: Stahl, Hoffman and Sauvages on Pathology," in *The Medical Enlightenment of the Eighteenth Century*, ed. by Andrew Cunningham and Roger French (New York, 1990), 97.

4. Guenter Risse, "Medicine in the Age of Enlightenment," in *History of Medicine in Society: Historical Essays*, ed. by A. Wear (Cambridge, 1992), 155–59.

5. Hays, *The Burdens of Disease*, 95–96.

6. Johanna Geyer-Kordesch, "Georg Ernst Stahl's Radical Pietist Medicine and Its Influence upon the German Enlightenment," in *The Medical Enlightenment of the Eighteenth Century*, ed. by Andrew Cunningham and Roger French (New York, 1990), 67–87.

7. French, "Sickness and the Soul," 103.

8. Hays, *The Burdens of Disease*, 99.

9. John A. Talbott, *A Biographical History of Medicine: Excerpts and Essays on the Men and Their Work* (New York, 1970), 126.

10. Roy Porter, "The Eighteenth Century," in *The Western Medical Tradition: 800 B.C. to A.D. 1800*, ed. by Lawrence I. Conrad, Michael Neve, Vivian Nutton, Roy Porter, and Andrew Wear (Cambridge, 1995), 453.

11. Eisenberg, "Disease and Illness," 11. Italics in the original.

12. Michel Foucault, *The Birth of the Clinic: An Archaeology of Medical Perception*, trans. by A. M. Sheridan Smith (New York, 1994), 109–10, passim.

13. Nestor Miranda Canal, "Apuntes para la historia de la medicina en Colombia," *Ciencia, Tecnología y Desarrollo* 8:1–2 (January–June 1984), 156.

14. John Jay TePaske, "José Celestino Mutis," in *Encyclopedia of Latin American History and Culture*, ed. by Barbara A. Tenenbaum, 5 vols. (New York, 1996), 5:150–51; Quevedo V., *Institucionalización de la medicina*, 100–112.

15. Soriano Lleras, *La medicina en la colonia*, 192, 199; Ibáñez, *Crónicas de Bogotá*, 119.

16. Ibid., 215.

17. Ibáñez, *Memorias*, 161.

18. Christopher Abel, *Health Care in Colombia, c. 1920–c. 1950: A Preliminary Analysis* (London, 1994), 10.

19. Soriano Lleras, *La medicina en la colonia*, 186–88.

20. Emilio Quevedo V., "José Celestino Mutis y la educación médica en el Nuevo Reino de Granada," *Ciencia, Tecnología y Desarrollo* 8:1–4 (January–December 1984), 74.

21. Hernando Forero Caballero, *Evolución histórica de la medicina en Santa Fe de Bogotá* (Bogotá, 1983), 90.

22. Soriano Lleras, *San Juan de Dios*, 27–29; Abel, *Health Care in Colombia*, 9; Quevedo V., *Institucionalización de la medicina*, 119–22.

23. Soriano Lleras, *La medicina en la colonia*, 265.

24. Ibáñez, *Memorias*, 54.

25. Ibid., 40; Soriano Lleras, *La medicina en la colonia*, 264–66.

26. Miranda Canal, "Apuntes," 4–5.

27. Guerra, "Medical Education," 444; Ibáñez, *Memorias*, 162–64; Abel, *Health Care in Colombia*, 12.

28. Miranda Canal, "Apuntes," 5; David Bushnell, *The Santander Regime in Gran Colombia* (Westport, CT, 1970), 190–91.

29. Soriano Lleras, *San Juan de Dios*, 38; El Estudiante [José Félix Merizalde], *El desengaño anatómico de 6 de Noviembre de 1824* (Bogotá, 1824).

30. Bernardo Daste, *Al público imparcial* (Bogotá, 1824).

31. José Félix Merizalde, *Contestación al Señor Bernardo Daste* (Bogotá, 1824).

32. Foucault, *The Birth of the Clinic*, passim.

33. Good, *Medicine, Rationality, and Experience*, 65, 71, 86.

34. Juan María Pardo, *Discurso pronunciado por el Señor Doctor Juan María Pardo a la Facultad de Medicina* (Bogotá, 1830), 2.

35. José Félix Merizalde, *El empírico de Bogotá* (Bogotá, 1824), 13, 56.

36. Soriano Lleras, *La medicina en la colonia*, 127–29; *El Album*, November 15, December 1, 1856.

37. *El Dia*, June 7, 1850.

38. *La Lanceta*, April 17, 1852.

39. Ibid.

40. Ibid., May 16, 1856.

41. Merizalde, *Contestación al Señor Bernardo Daste*, 11.

42. *La Lanceta*, April 17, 1852.

43. Ibid. Italics added.

44. Ibid., May 16, June 20, August 19, September 20, October 26, 1852.

45. Bushnell, *Making of Modern Colombia*, 101–24.

46. These physicians included Andrés María Pardo, Antonio Ospina, Francisco Bayón, Liborio Zerda, Rafael Rocha, Manuel A. Angel, Flavio Malo, W. L. Dudly, Joaquin Maldonado, Ignacio Antorvesa, Joaquin Sarmiento, Jorge Vargas, and Bernardo Medina. See Miranda Canal, "Apuntes," 164–65.

47. Ibáñez, *Memorias,* 155.

48. *Gaceta Médica de Bogotá*, March 24, 1865.

49. Ibid., January 18, 1865.

50. Miranda Canal, "Apuntes," 152–53, 157, 159–61.

51. Diana Obregón Torres, *Sociedades científicas en Colombia: La invención de una tradición, 1859–1936* (Bogotá, 1992), 41; Jane Meyer Loy, "Modernization and Educational Reform in Colombia, 1863–1886" (Ph.D. diss., University of Wisconsin, 1969), 223. Andrés M. Pardo, Antonio Ospina, Antonio Vargas Vega, Antonio Vargas Reyes, Bernardo Medina, José María Buendía, Librado Rivas, Manuel A. Angel, Manuel Plata Azuero, Nicolás Osorio, and Rafael Rocha C. occupied the chairs. See Ibáñez, *Memorias*, 112. Many of these men were involved in the Perdomo incident.

52. Norman Gevitz, "Unorthodox Medical Theories," in *Companion Encyclopedia of the History of Medicine*, ed. by W. F. Bynum and Roy Porter, 2 vols. (New York, 1993), 1:604–12; Manuel María Madiedo, *Un eco de Hahnemann en los Andes*

(Bogotá, 1863), 4–6; Salvador María Alvarez, *Manual de medicina homeopática*, 2nd ed. (Bogotá, 1890), 77–85.

53. Madiedo, *Un eco de Hahnemann*; *La homeopatia*, tomo 1 (Bogotá, 1874), 4–17. One long-lived homeopathic pharmacy, La Santa Rita, is located next door to the Biblioteca Luis Angel Arango.

54. *Revista de los Establecimientos de Beneficiencia*, November 24, 1870.

55. Quevedo V., *Institucionalización de la medicina*, 179.

56. Arcos, *Evolución de la medicina*, 159–63.

57. Guerra, "Medical Education," 438–39; Arcos, *Evolución de la medicina*, 147–63; Shaman, *Medicina y economía*, 156.

58. Alchon, *Native Society and Disease*, 108.

59. Ibáñez, *Memorias*, 207

60. Arcos, *Evolución de la medicina*, 217–18.

61. Shaman, *Medicina y economía*, 196–98.

62. Arcos, *Evolución de la medicina*, 256, 259–60, 264.

63. Juan José Samaniega, *Cronología médica ecuatoriana* (Quito, 1957), 168.

64. Arcos, *Evolución de la medicina*, 255.

65. Consejo Municipal de Quito, Copiador de Actas, Sesión 9 de Abril, 1867, Archivo Municipal de Historia (Quito) (hereafter AMHQ), 123–124f.

66. Consejo Municipal de Quito, Ministerio de Hacienda, 1867, AMHQ, 62–69.

67. Shaman, *Medicina y economía*, 199–200.

68. E. Gayraud and D. Domec, *La capital del Ecuador desde el punto de vista médico-quirúrgico*, trans. by Virgilio Paredes Borja (Quito, 1953, orig. pub. 1886), 19.

69. Obregón Torres, *Sociedades científicas*, 48; Miranda Canal, "Apuntes," 56.

70. *Reglamento de la Escuela de Medicina* (Bogotá, 1865).

71. Anales de la Universidad Nacional de los Estados Unidos de Colombia, *Repertoria de instrucción pública, literatura, filosofía, i ciencias matemáticas, físicas, médicas i legales*, Tomo1 [1 de Septiembre de 1868 a Septiembre de 1869] (Bogotá, 1868), 36, 54–55.

72. Fernando Uricoechea, "La institucionalización de la práctica científica en Colombia," *Ciencia, Tecnología y Desarrollo* 8:1–4 (1984), 54.

73. Forero Caballero, *Evolución histórica*, 89–90.

74. *Decreto acordado por la Camara de Provincia de Bogotá, arreglando el Hospital de Caridad* (Bogotá, 1840), 2–18.

75. Anales de la Universidad Nacional, *Repertoria*, 15–16.

76. Forero Caballero, *Evolución histórica*, 99.

77. Julián Vargas Lesmes and Guillermo Vera Pardo, "Formas asistenciales y de beneficencia en Santafé: Hospitales, expósitos y hospicios," in *La sociedad Santa Fé Colonial*, ed. by Julián Vargas Lesmes (Bogotá, 1990), 289–90.

78. Frank Safford, *The Ideal of the Practical: Colombia's Struggle to Form a Technical Elite* (Austin, TX, 1976), 57–62.

79. Ibáñez, *Crónicas de Bogotá*, 4:560.

80. *Revista de los Establecimientos de Beneficencia*, November 24, 1870, January 28, April 14, 1871, September 1, 1872.

81. Miranda Canal, "Apuntes," 6–7; Uricoechea, "La Institucionalización," 170; Abel, *Health Care in Colombia*, 14–15; Pablo García Medina, *El método experimental aplicado a la clinica médica* (Bogotá, 1897), 14.

82. Obregón Torres, *Sociedades científicas*, 51.

83. Ibid., 51–55.

84. Abel, *Health Care in Colombia*, 13.

85. Obregón Torres, *Sociedades científicas*, 53–55.

86. Ibid., 64–68.

87. República de Colombia, *Reglamento de la Academia Nacional de Medicina* (Bogotá, 1893), 16.

88. República de Colombia, *Congreso Médico Nacional: 20 de Julio de 1893* (Bogotá, 1892); Obregón Torres, *Sociedades científicas*, 65.

89. Agustín Albarracín Tevlón, "Intrusos, charlatanes, secretistas y curanderos: Aproximación sociológica al estudio de la asistencia médica extracientífica en la España del siglo XIX," *Asclepio* 24 (1972), 323–66.

90. William Duke Gibson, *The Constitutions of Colombia* (Durham, NC, 1948), 202, 320; Ibáñez, *Memorias*, 81, 87–88.

91. Gibson, *The Constitutions of Colombia*, 202, 320.

92. República de Colombia, *Leyes de la República de Colombia expedidas por el consejo nacional legislativo en sus sesiones de 1886* (Bogotá, 1887), 63–64.

93. República de Colombia, *Codificación de los decretos de caracter permanente dictado por el Poder Ejecutivo de 7 de Agosto de 1904 a Diciembre de 1905* (Bogotá, 1905), 616–18.

94. República de Colombia, *Leyes expedidas por el congreso nacional en su legislatura de año de 1914* (Bogotá, 1915), 179–85; República de Colombia, *Leyes expedidas por el congreso nacional en su legislatura de año de 1920* (Bogotá, 1921), 88–89.

95. Hector Pedraza M., *La enfermeria en Colombia: Reseña histórica sobre su desarrollo* (Bogotá, 1954), 21–22, 79–81, 89.

96. República de Colombia, *Legislación colombiana sobre higiene y sanidad* (Bogotá, 1937), 114–18; Alfredo Cardona Hernández, *La responsibilidad médica ante la ley* (Medellín, 1980), 299–303.

97. Pedraza M., *La enfermeria en Colombia*, 79–81.

98. Abel, *Health Care in Colombia*, 22.

99. Ibid., 16–17, 25.

100. Municipal Council Session, April 5, 1867, Consejo Municipal de Quito, Copiador de Actas, 1866–68, Secretaría, Fondo Histórico Documental, AMHQ, 119r-20.

101. *Reglamento de policia* (Quito, 1885), 91.

102. *Boletín del Sindicato Médico-Ecuatoriano* 1 (February 15, 1928).

Chapter 3, Pages 61–87

1. *El Tradicionista*, May 7, 1872.

2. *El Heraldo*, September 23, 1870.

3. *El Tradicionista*, May 7, 1872.

4. Madero Moreira, *Historia de la medicina*, 237; *El Diario de Cundinamarca*, May 11, 1872; *La Ilustración*, February 19, 1875. José María Cordovez Moure relates that many towns claimed to be Perdomo's birthplace. He favors Totorí, in the Cauca, as the most likely site. See his *Reminiscencias*, 7:364. See also *La Ilustración*, February 19, 1875.

5. The Conservative and Liberal parties, both of which coalesced in the 1840s, dominate much of Colombian political history. The ideological differences between the two parties are often quite small. The names of the parties are capitalized throughout the text, but references to a related ideology, such as liberalism, are lowercased.

6. Bushnell, *The Making of Modern Colombia*, 120–26.

7. *El Diario de Cundinamarca*, May 13, 1872.

8. Ibid., May 13, 1872, April 26, 1873; *El Tradicionista*, May 7, 1872; Cordovez Moure, *Reminiscencias*, 7:347–48.

9. This point is analyzed in great detail in Taussig, *Shamanism, Colonialism, and the Wild Man*.

10. *La Ilustración*, February 19, 1875; Virgilio Parédes Borja, *Historia de la medicina en el Ecuador*, 2 vols. (Quito, 1963), 1:265–66; Madero Moreira, *Historia de la medicina*, 237.

11. Miguel Perdomo Neira, *La iglesia católica en presencia del siglo XIX* (Bogotá, 1872), 110.

12. Ibid., 109–10.

13. Perdomo Neira, "Al público," February 1867, in Perdomo Neira, *La iglesia católica*, 111.

14. Cordovez Moure, *Reminiscencias*, 7:350, 353.

15. Ibid., 348, 376–77.

16. *La Ilustración*, May 21, 1872.

17. Ibid., April 9, 1872.

18. *La Ilustración*, June 4, 1872; *El Diario de Cundinamarca*, May 13, 21, 1872.

19. *La América Latina*, November 7, 1866.

20. Ibid.

21. Ibid.

22. Perdomo Neira, "Al público," in Perdomo Neira, *La iglesia católica*, 111.

23. *La América Latina*, November 14, 1866.

24. *Un ultraje inmerecido* (Quito, 1867). Dozens of other testimonials are recorded in *La iglesia católica*, 114–43.

25. *Un ultraje inmerecido*.

26. Unos reconocidos, "El Señor Perdomo," Quito, October 26, 1867, in Perdomo Neira, *La iglesia católica*, 114–16.

27. Mil enfermos, "Al gobierno i la facultad médica," Quito, November 8, 1867, in Perdomo Neira, *La iglesia católica*, 116–17.

28. Perdomo Neira, "La verdad manifestada," Quito, December 4, 1867, in Perdomo Neira, *La iglesia católica*, 120.

29. These leaders included Manuel Tovar (head of the council), Dr. Nicolás Egas, Vicente Cisneros, Carlos Auz, Francisco Miranda, Julio Portilla, and Juan Fabara.

30. *Reglamento de la policia formado para la provincia de Quito* (Quito, 1842), 1.

31. Parédes Borja, *Historia de la medicina en el Ecuador*, 1:265–66; Madero Moreira, *Historia de la medicina*, 237; Pablo Bustamante to President, Consejo Municipal, December 7, 1867, AMHQ, Fondo Histórico Documental, Sección Secretaría, Serie: Oficios y Solicitudes Dirigidas al Presidente del Consejo, 2:1867, no. 196ff, 721–22.

32. Bustamante to President, AMHQ, November 20, 1867, folio 696.

33. *Un ultraje inmerecido.*

34. La humanidad indolente, "Boletín de Sanidad Numero 1º," Quito, December 11, 1867, in Perdomo Neira, *La iglesia católica*, 126.

35. La humanidad doliente, "Boletín de Sanidad Numero 2º," Quito, December 11, 1867, in Perdomo Neira, *La iglesia católica*, 129–33.

36. *Los Andes* (Quito), December 14, 1867.

37. Sesión de Consejo, December 12, 1867, AMHQ, Copiador de Actas, 1866–1868, tomo 573-A, folios 229–30.

38. Leandro M. Pulido, "El Doctor Miguel Perdomo Neira," Neiva, August 10, 1869, in Perdomo Neira, *La iglesia católica*, 148–63.

39. "Venta de hacienda," Notaría de Popayán, 1869, Archivo Central del Cauca (hereafter ACC), vol. 1, folios 645–47.

40. Instituto Geográfico "Agustín Codazzi," *Diccionario geográfico de Colombia*, 2 vols. (Bogotá, 1971), 1:216.

41. "Venta de hacienda," 1871, ACC, vol. 1, folios 531–34.

42. "Venta de terreno," 1871, ACC, vol. 1, folios 540–42, 546–48.

43. "Comunicaciones con el distrito de Cajibio," Manos Muertos, 1871, ACC, legajo 73, folio 115.

44. "Protocolización de bienes de Miguel Perdomo Neira," Notaría de Popayán, 1881, ACC, vol. 1, folios 261–67.

45. *El Diario de Cundinamarca*, April 26, 1873.

46. *El Heraldo*, June 16, 1870.

47. *Godo* was a derisive name for Conservatives, implying retrograde mentality.

48. Leandro M. Pulido, "El Doctor Miguel Perdomo Neira," in Perdomo Neira, *La iglesia católica*, 148–63.

49. *El Heraldo*, September 16, 1870.

50. Ibid., September 16, 1870.

51. *La Ilustración*, May 7, 1872; *El Diario de Cundinamarca*, April 26, 1873.

52. Octavio Arizmendi Posada, "Historicidad de los hechos extraordinarios ocurridas en Chiquinquira en 1586," in *Chiquinquira: 400 años*, ed. by Octavio Arizmendi Posada (Bogotá, 1986), 13, 25–26.

53. J. León Helquera, "Chiquinquira," in *Encyclopedia of Latin American History and Culture*, ed. by Barbara A. Tenenbaum, 5 vols. (New York, 1996), 2:143.

54. These men were part of the Antioqueño wing of the Conservative party and used the paper to engage in polemics with the Conservative Miguel Antonio Caro (of *El Tradicionista*) and the Liberal editors of *El Diario de Cundinamarca*. See Jesús Alvarez and Ma. Teresa Uribe de H., preparers, *Indice de prensa colombiana, 1840–1890: Periódicos existentes en la Biblioteca Central* (Medellín, 1984), 145.

55. *La Ilustración*, April 9, 1872.

56. Ibid., April 9, May 4, 7, 8, 21, 1872.

57. Cordovez Moure, *Reminiscencias*, 7:369–70.

58. *El Tradicionista*, May 7, 1872.

59. *La Ilustración*, May 4, 7, 1872; Cordovez Moure, *Reminiscencias*, 7:352.

60. *La Ilustración*, May 7, 1872.

61. Cordovez Moure, *Reminiscencias*, 7:352.

62. *La Ilustración*, May 4, 1872; Cordovez Moure, *Reminiscencias*, 7:354.

63. *El Diario de Cundinamarca*, May 7, 1872.

64. Ibid., May 8, 1872; Cordovez Moure, *Reminiscencias*, 7:355.

65. *La Ilustración*, May 7, 1872.

66. Ibid., May 8, 1872.

67. Ibid.

68. Ibid., May 14, 1872.

69. *El Tradicionista*, May 14, 1872.

70. Cordovez Moure, *Reminiscencias*, 7:357–59.

71. *El Tradicionista*, May 14, 1872; *La Ilustración*, May 14, June 4, 1872.

72. Cordovez Moure, *Reminiscencias*, 7:361.

73. *La Ilustración*, May 14, 16, 1872; Cordovez Moure, *Reminiscencias*, 7:361–62, 366.

74. *La Ilustración*, June 4, 1872.

75. Ibid., May 14, 1872; Cordovez Moure, *Reminiscencias*, 7:366–67.

76. *El Diario de Cundinamarca*, June 8, 1872.

77. Ibid., June 15, 1872.

78. *La Ilustración*, May 16, 1872.

79. *El Bien Público* (Bogotá), May 21, 1872.

80. *El Tradicionista*, May 18, 1872; Cordovez Moure, *Reminiscencias*, 7:362–63.

81. *La Ilustración*, May 16, 1872.

82. Ibid., May 21, 1872.

83. Ibid., May 14, 1872.

84. Ibid., May 23, 1872.

85. *El Diario de Cundinamarca*, May 13, 1872.

86. Ibid., May 21, 1872.

87. José María Samper and José María Quijano Otero edited the paper. Contributors included Joaquín Posada, Indalecio Liévano, Soledad Acosta de Samper, Juan Buenaventura Ortiz, Carlos Holquín, Agustín Núñez, Camilo Antonio Echeverri, and Demetrio Viana. See Alvarez and Uribe, *Indice de prensa colombiana*, 45.

88. *El Bien Público* (Bogotá), May 21, 1872.

89. *El Diario de Cundinamarca*, May 21, 1872.

90. David Sowell, " 'La teoría i la realidad': The Democratic Society of Artisans of Bogotá, 1847–1854," *Hispanic American Historical Review* 67:4 (November 1987), 611–30.

91. *La Ilustración*, June 1, 1872.

92. Ibid., June 4, 1872.

93. Ibid.

94. Ibid.

95. Ibid., June 13, 1872.

96. Ibid.

97. *El Diario de Cundinamarca*, July 16, 1873.

98. Cordovez Moure, *Reminiscencias*, 7:367–70.

99. *El Diario de Cundinamarca*, April 26, 1873.

100. *La Ilustración*, February 19, 1875.

101. The Escuela Politécnico opened in October 1870 under Jesuit leadership, several months after Sodiro, Teodoro Wolf, and Juan Bautista Menten arrived from Europe. Sodiro, who had been born in Venice in 1836, became one of Ecuador's leading botanists. After the school closed in 1876, he withdrew from the Jesuit order and remained in Ecuador until his death in 1909. See César Bustes-Videla, "Church and State in Ecuador: A History of Politico-Ecclesiastical Relations during the Age of Gabriel García Moreno, 1860–1875" (Ph.D. diss., Georgetown University, 1966), 176–80, 182, 185. Sodiro's publications apparently do not mention either *alizá* or Perdomo. See Luis Sodiro, *Contribuciones al conocimiento de la flora ecuatoriana* (Quito, 1900), and idem, *Una excursión botánica* (Quito, 1881).

102. Madero Moreira, *Historia de la medicina*, 237–38.

103. Samaniego, *Cronología médica ecuatoriana*, 211.

104. Madero Moreira, *Historia de la medicina*, 238; *La Ilustración*, February 19, 1875.

Chapter 4, Pages 89–109

1. Diana Obregón Torres, "Struggling against Leprosy: Physicians, Medicine, and Society in Colombia, 1880–1940" (Ph.D. diss., Virginia Polytechnic Institute and State University, 1997).

2. A phrase in the Hmong language of Southeast Asia. See Anne Fadiman, *The Spirit Catches You and You Fall Down: A Hmong Child, Her American Doctors, and the Collision of Two Cultures* (New York, 1997).

3. Gutiérrez de Pineda, *Medicina tradicional de Colombia*, 2:26.

4. Viesca Treviño, "La medicina tradicional mexicana," 14–15.

5. Jacqueline Clarac de Briceño, *La enfermedad como lenguaje en Venezuela* (Merida, Venezuela, 1992), 75–79. See also Angelina Pollak-Eltz, *La medicina popular en Venezuela* (Caracas, 1987).

6. Arthur Kleinman, *Patients and Healers in the Context of Culture: An Exploration of the Borderland between Anthropology, Medicine, and Psychiatry* (Berkeley, CA, 1980), 24–60, as cited in Tedlock, "Humoral Medicine in Latin America," 1071.

7. Gutiérrez de Pineda, *Medicina tradicional de Colombia*, 26; M. de la Luz Alvarez, M. Teresa Araneda, Elisa Fiqueroa, Soledad Osorio, "Tratamiento de enfermedades en una población rural: ¿Vigencia de elementos hispánicos?" *Social Science and Medicine* 17:8 (1983), 471–74.

8. Charles Stuart Cochrane, *Journal of a Residence and Travels in Colombia during the Years 1823 and 1824*, 2 vols. (London, 1825), 2:9.

9. Obregón Torres, *Sociedades científicas*, 68; Abel, *Health Care in Colombia*, 13–14.

10. Uribe Angel, *La medicina en Antioquia*, 82.

11. David Arnold, *Imperial Medicine and Indigenous Responses*, as cited in Shula Marks, "What Is Colonial about Colonial Medicine? And What Has Happened to Imperialism and Health?" *Journal of the Social History of Medicine* 10:2 (1997), 206.

12. Robert M. Levine, *Vale of Tears: Revisiting the Canudos Massacre in Northeastern Brazil, 1893–1897* (Berkeley, CA, 1992).

13. Paul J. Vanderwood, *The Power of God against the Guns of Government: Religious Upheaval in Mexico at the Turn of the Nineteenth Century* (Stanford, CA, 1998).

14. June Macklin, "Belief, Ritual, and Healing: New England Spiritualism and Mexican-American Spiritism Compared," in *Religious Movements in Contemporary America*, ed. by Irving I. Zacesty and Mark P. Leon (Princeton, NJ, 1974), 383–87. See also David J. Hess, *Spirits and Scientists: Ideology, Spiritism, and Brazilian Culture* (University Park, PA, 1991).

15. José Peregrino Sanmiguel contributed several pieces to this polemic. See his *Carta primera* (Bogotá, 1866), *La medicina homeopática (Carta segunda)* (Bogotá, 1866), *Homeopatía* (Bogotá, 1867), *Carta cuarta* (Bogotá, 1867), and *Polémica homeopática (Carta quinta)* (Bogotá, 1869). See also María del Pilar Guzmán Urrea, "La alopatía y la homeopatía en el siglo XIX: Conflicto entre dos prácticas médicas," *Anuario Colombiano de Historia Social y de la Cultura* 22 (1995), 59–73.

16. Madiedo, *Un eco de Hahnemann*, 23.

17. *Gaceta Médica de Bogotá*, November 15, 1864.

18. *La Homeopatía*, 116, 232–33, 250, 253.

19. Madiedo, *Un eco de Hahnemann*, 4, 24.

20. Perdomo Neira, *La iglesia católica*, 5, 91, 97, 111.

21. Leandro M. Pulido, "El Doctor Miguel Perdomo Neira," Nieva, August 10, 1869, in Perdomo Neira, *La iglesía Católica*, 148–49.

22. Rivas, "Perdomo," 224.

23. Ibid.

24. *El Diario de Cundinamarca*, April 26, 1873.

25. Ibid.

26. Ibid.

27. Sergio Arboleda, *Las ciencias, las letras y las bellas artes en Colombia* (Bogotá, 1936), 53–55, 62–63; Martín Alonso Pinzón, *Historia del conservatismo* (Bogotá, 1979), 190.

28. Ricardo de la Parra, "¿Quien es el Señor Miguel Perdomo Neira?" in Perdomo Neira, *La iglesía católica*, 193.

29. Perdomo Neira, *La iglesia católica*, 77–80.

30. *La Caridad*, cited in *La Verdad* (Quito), July 24, 1874.

31. *La Verdad*, November 18, 1872.

32. Perdomo Neira, *La iglesia católica*, 91–93.

33. Unos reconocidos, "El Señor Perdomo," Quito, October 26, 1867, in Perdomo Neira, *La iglesía católica*, 114.

34. Setha M. Low, "The Medicalization of Healing Cults in Latin America," *American Ethnologist* 15:1 (February 1988), 137.

35. June Macklin, "Two Faces of Sainthood: The Pious and the Popular," *Journal of Latin American Lore* 14:1 (1988), 69.

36. Kathleen L. Figgen, "Miracles and Promises: Popular Religious Cults and Saints in Argentina" (Ph.D. diss., Indiana University, 1990), 60–61, 70.

37. Octavio Ignacio Romano V., "Charismatic Medicine, Folk-Healing, and Folk-Sainthood," *American Anthropologist* 67 (1965), 1151–73.

38. Vanderwood, *The Power of God*, 162.

39. Macklin, "Belief, Ritual, and Healing," passim.

40. Levine, *Vale of Tears*, passim.

41. De la Parra, "¿Quien es el Señor Miguel Perdomo Neira?" in Perdomo Neira, *La iglesia católica*, 193.

42. Luise Margolies, "José Gregorio Hernández: The Historical Development of a Venezuelan Popular Saint," *Studies in Latin American Popular Culture* 3 (1984), 28–46.

43. Luise Margolies, "Promises and Pilgrimages: Religious Devotion to José Gregorio Hernández in Venezuela," *Actas del XLI Congreso Internacional de Americanistas* 3, as cited in Setha M. Low, "The Medicalization of Healing Cults in Latin America," *American Ethnologist* 15:1 (February 1988), 143.

44. Luise Margolies, "The Canonization of a Venezuelan Folk Saint: The Case of José Gregorio Hernández," *Journal of Latin American Lore* 14:1 (1988), 93–110.

45. Taussig, *Shamanism, Colonialism, and the Wild Man*, 147, 149, 273, 279–81; Low, "Medicalization of Healing Cults," 142–45.

46. Setha M. Low, "Dr. Moreno Cañas: A Symbolic Bridge to the Demedicalization of Healing," *Social Science and Medicine* 16:5 (1982), 527; idem, "Medicalization of Healing Cults in Latin America," 130–42.

47. Manco Silverio, *La doctrina de la Madre María: Cómo la difundía para curar las enfermedades del cuerpo y del alma (consideraciones científicas)* (Buenos Aires, 1974).

48. June Macklin, "Folk Saints, Healers and Spiritist Cults in Northern Mexico," *Revista/Review Interamericana* 3 (1974), 351–67.

49. Seth Leacock and Ruth Leacock, *Spirits of the Deep: A Study of an Afro-Brazilian Cult* (Garden City, NJ, 1972), 250–84.

50. Sidney M. Greenfield, "The Return of Dr. Fritz: Spiritist Healing and Patronage Networks in Urban, Industrial Brazil," *Social Science and Medicine* 24:12 (1987), 1095–1108. See also Diana Jean Schemo, "Live, in Brazil (Again): The Reincarnated Dr. Fritz," *New York Times*, January 12, 1996, A4, and Kaja Finkler, *Spiritualist Healers in Mexico: Successes and Failures of Alternative Therapeutics*, foreword by Arthur Kleinman (New York, 1985).

51. Pedersen and Baruffati, "Healers, Dieties, Saints and Doctors," 492; Low, "Dr. Moreno Cañas," passim; Leacock, *Spirits of the Deep*.

52. Pedersen and Baruffati, "Healers, Dieties, Saints and Doctors," 492.

53. Low, "Dr. Moreno Cañas," 527.

54. Taussig, *Shamanism, Colonialism, and the Wild Man*, 281.

55. Irwin Press, "The Urban Curandero," *American Anthropologist* 73 (1971), 742–56. For a description of medical choices available in a Guatemalan Mayan community, see Robert Ness, Gretel H. Pelto, and Pertti J. Pelto, "Alternative Curing Strategies in a Changing Medical Situation," *Medical Anthropology* 3 (Summer 1977), 25–54.

56. Ronald Frankenberg, "Medical Anthropology and Development: A Theoretical Perspective," *Social Science and Medicine* 14B:3 (1980), 197–207.

57. Janzen, "Comparative Study of Medical Systems," 124.

58. Ibid., 127–29.

59. Macklin, "Folk Saints, Healers and Spiritist Cults," 301; Press, "Classification of Medical Systems," 47; Crandon-Malamud, *From the Fat of Our Souls*.

60. Viesca Treviño, "La medicina tradicional mexicana," 19.

61. Eisenberg, "Disease and Illness," 9–11.

62. Gregory Pappas, "Some Implications for the Study of the Doctor/Patient Interaction: Power, Structure, and Agency in the Works of Howard Waitzkin and Arthur Kleinman," *Social Science and Medicine* 30:2 (1990), 202.

63. Eisenberg, "Disease and Illness," 19–21. Eisenberg notes that for some biomedical doctors, the word "placebo" is often an "epithet suggesting charlatanism."

64. Viesca Treviño, "La medicina tradicional mexicana," 21.

BIBLIOGRAPHY

Primary Sources

Archives

Archivo Central del Cauca (ACC): Manos Muertos, Notaría de Popayán

Archivo Municipal de Historia (Quito) (AMHQ): Sección Secretaría, Copiador de Actas; Ministerio de Hacienda, Oficios y Solicitudes Dirigidas al Presidente del Consejo

Newspapers

El Album (Bogotá)
La América Latina (Quito)
Los Andes (Guayaquil)
Los Andes (Quito)
El Bien Público (Bogotá)
El Bien Público (Guayaquil)
Boletín del Sindicato Médico-Ecuatoriano (Quito)
El Dia (Bogotá)
El Diario de Cundinamarca (Bogotá)
El Ecuador (Quito)
La Estrella de Mayo (Quito)
Gaceta Médica de Bogotá (Bogotá)
El Heraldo (Medellín)
La Ilustración (Bogotá)

La Lanceta (Bogotá)
New York Times (New York)
La Nueva Era (Guayaquil)
El Porvenir Nacional (Guayaquil)
La Prensa (Guayaquil)
Revista de los Establecimientos de Beneficencia (Bogotá)
El Tradicionista (Bogotá)
La Verdad (Quito)

Pamphlets and Official Documents

Daste, Bernardo. *Al público imparcial.* Bogotá: Imprenta de Espinosa, por Valentin Rodriguez Molano, 1824.

Decreto acordado por la Camara de Provincia de Bogotá, arreglando el Hospital de Caridad. Bogotá: Imprenta por José Antonio Cualla, 1840.

El Estudiante [José Félix Merizalde]. *El desengaño anatómico de 6 de Noviembre de 1824.* Bogotá: Imprenta de Espinosa, por Valentin Rodriguez Molano, 1824.

La homeopatía. Bogotá: Imprenta de Foción Mantilla, 1874.

Merizalde, José Félix. *Contestación al Señor Bernardo Daste.* Bogotá: Imprenta de Espinosa, por Valentin Rodriguez Molano, 1824.

——. *El empírico de Bogotá.* Bogotá: Impreso de Espinosa, por V. R. Molano, 1824.

Ministerio de Educación Nacional. División de Documentación y Fomento Bibliotecario. *Catálogo de tesis de la región central: Ciencias biomédicas.* Bogotá: Instituto Colombiano para el Fomento de la Educación Superior, 1976.

Pardo, Juan María. *Discurso pronunciado por el Señor Doctor Juan María Pardo a la Facultad de Medicina.* Bogotá: Imprenta de B. Espinosa, por José Ayarza, 1830.

Peregrino Sanmiguel, José. *Carta cuarta.* Bogotá: Imprenta de F. Mantilla, 1867.

——. *Carta primera.* Bogotá: Imprenta de F. Mantilla, 1866.

——. *Homeopatía.* Bogotá: Imprenta de F. Mantilla, 1867.

_____. *La medicina homeopática (Carta segunda)*. Bogotá: Imprenta de F. Mantilla, 1866.

_____. *Polémica homeopática*. Bogotá: Imprenta de Gaitán, 1869.

Reglamento de la Escuela de Medicina. Bogotá: Imprenta Constitucional, 1865.

Reglamento de la policía. Quito: Imprenta Nacional, 1885.

Reglamento de la policía formado para la provincia de Quito. Quito: Imprenta de Alvarado, 1842.

República de Colombia. *Codificación de los decretos de caracter permanente dictado por el Poder Ejecutivo de 7 de Agosto de 1904 a Diciembre de 1905*. Bogotá: Imprenta Nacional, 1905.

_____. *Congreso Médico Nacional: 20 de Julio de 1893*. Bogotá: Imprenta de "La Luz," 1892.

_____. *Legislación colombiana sobre higiene y sanidad*. Bogotá: Editorial de la Lit. Colombia, 1937.

_____. *Leyes de la República de Colombia expedidas por el consejo nacional legislativo en sus sesiones de 1886*. Bogotá: Imprenta de Vapor de Zalamea Hermanos, 1887.

_____. *Leyes expedidas por el congreso nacional en su legislatura de año de 1914*. Bogotá: Imprenta Nacional, 1915.

_____. *Leyes expedidas por el congreso nacional en su legislatura de año de 1920*. Bogotá: Imprenta Nacional, 1920.

_____. *Reglamento de la Academia Nacional de Medicina*. Bogotá: Imprenta de "La Luz," 1893.

Un ultraje inmerecido. Quito: Oficina Tipográfica de F. Bermeo, por J. Mora, December 5, 1867.

Secondary Sources

Abel, Christopher. *Health Care in Colombia, c. 1920–c. 1950: A Preliminary Analysis*. London: Institute of Latin American Studies, 1994.

Albarracín Tevlón, Agustín. "Intrusos, charlatanes, secretistas y curanderos: Aproximación sociológica al estudio de la asistencia médica extracientífica en la España del siglo XIX." *Asclepio* 24 (1972): 323–66.

_____. "La medicina española de los siglos XVI, XVII, y XVIII y su influencia en Colombia." *Cuadernos Hispanoamericanos* 472 (October 1989): 31–41.

Alchon, Suzanne Austin. *Native Society and Disease in Colonial Ecuador.* New York: Cambridge University Press, 1991.

Alcocer Andalón, Alberto. *Historia de la Escuela de Medicina de la Universidad Autónoma de San Luis Potosí.* Mexico City: Aconcagua Ediciones y Publicaciones, 1976.

Allen, Catherine. "Body and Soul in Quechua Thought." *Journal of Latin American Lore* 8 (1982): 179–96.

Alvarez, Jesús, and Ma. Teresa Uribe de H., preparers. *Indice de prensa colombiana, 1840–1890: Periódicos existentes en la Biblioteca Central.* Medellín: Sección de Documentación, Departamento de Bibliotecas, Universidad de Antioquia, 1984.

Alvarez, Salvador María. *Manual de medicina homeopática.* 2nd ed. Bogotá: Imprenta de Lleras, 1890.

Alvarez C., Julio. *Historia de la medicina tropical ecuatoriana.* 3 vols. Guayaquil: Editorial Arquidiocesana Justicia y Paz, 1980–1984.

Amaya P., Carolina, and Germán Zuluaga R. "Uso de purgantes en la medicina tradicional colombiana." *Interciencia* 16:6 (November–December 1991): 322–28.

Anales de la Universidad Nacional de los Estados Unidos de Colombia. *Repertoria de instrucción pública, literatura, filosofía, i ciencias matemáticas, físicas, médicas i legales.* Tomo 1 [1 de Septiembre de 1868 a Septiembre de 1869]. Bogotá: Imprenta de Echeverria Hermanos, 1868.

Anzures y Bolaños, María del Carmen. "Medicinas tradicionales y antropología." *Anales de Antropología* (Mexico City) 15 (1978): 131–64.

_____. *La medicina tradicional en México: Proceso histórico, sincretismos y conflictos.* Mexico City: Universidad Nacional Autónoma de México, 1983.

Arboleda, Sergio. *Las ciencias, las letras y las bellas artes en Colombia.* Bogotá: Editorial Minerva, 1936.

Archivo Nacional de Historia. *Guía del Archivo Nacional de Historia.* Quito: Editorial Casa de la Cultura Ecuatoriana, 1981.

Arcos, Gualberto. *Evolución de la medicina en el Ecuador.* 3rd ed. Quito: Editorial Casa de la Cultura Ecuatoriano, 1979.

_____. *La medicina en el Ecuador.* Quito: Tipográfico L. I. Fernández, 1933.

Arizmendi Posada, Octavio. "Historicidad de los hechos extraordinarios ocurridas en Chiquinquira en 1586." In *Chiquinquira: 400 años,* edited by Octavio Arizmendi Posada, 13–27. Bogotá: Fondo Cultural Cafetero, 1986.

Arriaga, Pablo Joseph de. *The Extirpation of Idolatry in Peru.* Translated and edited by L. Clark Keating. Lexington: University of Kentucky Press, 1968.

Asociación Colombiana de Facultades de Medicina. *Indice de la literatura médica colombiana, 1890–1960.* Bogotá: Ediciones Tercer Mundo, 1965.

Assadourian, Carlos Sempat. "Dominio colonial y señores étnicos en el espacio andino." *HISLA* (Lima) 1 (1983): 7–20.

Astudillo Espinosa, Celin. *Paginas históricas de la medicina ecuatoriana.* Quito: Instituto Panamericano de Geografía e Historia, 1981.

Barbier, Jacques A., and Lynda DeForest Craig. "Lepers and Hospitals in the Spanish Empire: An Aspect of Bourbon Reform in Health Care." *Ibero-Amerikanisches Archiv* 11:4 (1985): 383–406.

Barrett, Elinore M. "Indian Community Hospitals in Colonial Michoacán." In *Historical Geography of Latin America: Papers in Honor of Robert C. West,* edited by William V. Davidson and James J. Parsons, 83–96. Baton Rouge: Louisiana State University Press, 1980.

Bastien, Joseph William. "Differences between Kallawaya-Andean and Greek-European Humoral Theory." *Social Science and Medicine* 28:1 (1989): 45–51.

_____. *Healers of the Andes: Kallawaya Herbalists and Their Medicinal Plants.* Salt Lake City: University of Utah Press, 1987.

Basto Girón, Luis J. *Salud y enfermedad en el campesino del siglo XVIII.* Lima: Universidad Nacional Mayor de San Marcos, Seminario de Historia Rural Andina, 1977.

Behar, Ruth. "Sexual Witchcraft, Colonialism, and Women's Powers: Views from the Mexican Inquisition." In *Sexuality and Marriage in Colonial Latin America,* edited by Asunción Lavrin, 178–206. Lincoln: University of Nebraska Press, 1989.

Bove, Wilfredo. *El médico del hogar tratado popular de plantas medicinales.* Mexico City: Editora y Distribuidora Mexicana, 1977.

Brown, Michael Forbes. "Shamanism and Its Discontents." *Medical Anthropology Quarterly* 2:2 (June 1988): 102–20.

Brown, Peter. *The Cult of the Saints: Its Rise and Function in Latin Christianity.* Chicago: University of Chicago Press, 1981.

Burkholder, Mark A., and Lyman L. Johnson. *Colonial Latin America.* 2nd ed. New York: Oxford University Press, 1994.

Bushnell, David. *The Making of Modern Colombia: A Nation in Spite of Itself.* Berkeley: University of California Press, 1993.

———. *The Santander Regime in Gran Colombia.* Westport, CT: Greenwood Press, 1970.

Bustes-Videla, César. "Church and State in Ecuador: A History of Politico-Ecclesiastical Relations during the Age of Gabriel García Moreno, 1860–1875." Ph.D. diss., Georgetown University, 1966.

Bynum, W. F., and Roy Porter. *Companion Encyclopedia of the History of Medicine.* 2 vols. New York: Routledge, 1993.

Cardona Hernández, Alfredo. *La responsibilidad médica ante la ley.* Medellín: Editorial Copiyepes, 1980.

Chávez Velasquez, Nancy A. *La materia médica en el Incanato.* Lima: Editorial Mejia Baca, 1977.

Clarac de Briceño, Jacqueline. *La enfermedad como lenguaje en Venezuela.* Merida: CP, Universidad de los Andes, 1992.

Clavijo y Clavijo, Salvador. *La obra de la orden hospitalaria de San Juan de Dios en América y Filipinas.* Madrid: Artes Gráficas ARGES, 1950.

Cochrane, Charles Stuart. *Journal of a Residence and Travels in Colombia during the Years 1823 and 1824.* 2 vols. London: Henry Colburn, 1825.

Cock, Guillermo. "Sacerdotes o chamanes en el mundo andino." *Historia y Cultura* (Lima) 16 (1983): 135–46.

Cordovez Moure, José María. *Reminiscencias—Santa Fé y Bogotá.* 6th ed. 9 vols. Bogotá: Biblioteca Popular de Cultura Colombiana, 1942.

Cosminsky, Sheila. "Alimento and Fresco: Nutritional Concepts and Their Implications for Health Care." *Human Organization* 36:2 (Summer 1977): 203–7.

_____. "Changing Food and Medical Beliefs and Practices in a Guatemalan Community." *Ecology of Food and Nutrition* 4 (1975): 183–91.

Cosminsky, Sheila, and Ira E. Harrison. *Traditional Medicine*, Vol . 2, *1976–1981: Current Research with Implications for Ethnomedicine, Ethnopharmacology, Maternal and Child Health, Mental Health, and Public Health—An Annotated Bibliography of Africa, Latin America, and the Caribbean.* New York: Garland, 1984.

Cosminsky, Sheila, and M. Scrimshaw. "Medical Pluralism on a Guatemalan Plantation." *Social Science and Medicine* 14B:4 (November 1980): 267–78.

Crandon, Libbet. "Medical Dialogue and the Political Economy of Medical Pluralism: A Case from Rural Highland Bolivia." *American Ethnologist* 13:3 (August 1986): 463–76.

Crandon-Malamud, Libbet. *From the Fat of Our Souls: Social Change, Political Process, and Medical Pluralism in Bolivia.* Berkeley: University of California Press, 1991.

Custred, Glynn. "Inca Concepts of Soul and Spirit." In *Essays in Humanistic Anthropology*, edited by Bruce Grindal and Dennis Warren, 277–302. Washington, DC: University Press of America, 1979.

Davidson, Judith. "The Survival of Traditional Medicine in a Peruvian *Barriada.*" *Social Science and Medicine* 17:17 (1983): 1271–80.

Diccionario de historia eclesiástica de España. 4 vols. Madrid: Instituto Enríque Florez, 1972.

Dobkin de Rios, Marlene. "The Vidente Phenomenon in Third World Traditional Healing." *Medical Anthropology Quarterly* 8:1 (Winter 1984): 60–70.

Eisenberg, Leon. "Disease and Illness: Distinctions between Professional and Popular Ideas of Sickness." *Culture, Medicine and Psychiatry* 1:1 (1977): 9–23.

Eliade, Mircea. *Shamanism: Archaic Techniques of Ecstasy.* Translated by Willard R. Trask. Princeton, NJ: Princeton University Press, 1972.

Enciclopedia de la religión católica. 7 vols. Barcelona: Dalmau y Jover, S.A., 1951.

Estrella, Eduardo. *Medicina aborigen: La práctica médica aborigen de la sierra ecuatoriana.* Quito: Editorial Epoca, 1978.

Fabrega, Horacio, and Peter Manning. "An Integrated Theory of Disease: Landino-Mestizo Views of Disease in Chiapas Highlands." *Psychosomatic Medicine* 35 (1973): 223–39.

Fadiman, Anne. *The Spirit Catches You and You Fall Down: A Hmong Child, Her American Doctors, and the Collision of Two Cultures.* New York: Farrar, Straus and Giroux, 1997.

Figgen, Kathleen L. "Miracles and Promises: Popular Religious Cults and Saints in Argentina." Ph.D. diss., Indiana University, 1990.

Finkler, Kaja. *Spritualist Healers in Mexico: Successes and Failures of Alternative Therapeutics.* New York: Bergin and Garvey, 1985.

Ford, R. I. *The Nature and Status of Ethnobotany.* Ann Arbor: Museum of Anthropology, University of Michigan, 1978.

Forero Caballero, Hernando. *Evolución histórica de la medicina en Santa Fe de Bogotá.* Bogotá: Biblioteca de Autores Cundinamarquesas, 1983.

Foster, George M. "Hippocrates' Latin American Legacy: 'Hot and Cold' in Contemporary Folk Medicine." In *Colloquia in Anthropology,* edited by R. K. Wetherington, 3–19. Dallas, TX: Southern Methodist University Press, 1978.

_____. *Hippocrates' Latin American Legacy: Humoral Medicine in the New World.* Langhorne, PA: Gordon and Breach Science Publishers, 1994.

_____. *Humoral Pathology in Spain and Spanish America.* Madrid: Homenaje a Julio Caro Baroja, 1978.

_____. "On the Origin of Humoral Medicine in Latin America." *Medical Anthropology Quarterly* 1:4 (December 1987): 355–93.

_____. "On the Origin of Humoral Medicine in Latin American Traditional Spanish-American Therapeutics." *American Ethnologist* 15:1 (February 1988): 120–35.

_____. "The Validating Role of Humoral Theory in Traditional Spanish-American Therapeutics." *American Ethnologist* 15:1 (February 1988): 120–35.

Foucault, Michel. *The Birth of the Clinic: An Archaeology of Medical Perception.* Translated by A. M. Sheridan Smith. New York: Vintage Books, 1994.

Frankenberg, Ronald. "Medical Anthropology and Development: A Theoretical Perspective." *Social Science and Medicine* 14B:3 (1980): 197–207.

French, Roger. "Sickness and the Soul: Stahl, Hoffman and Sauvages on Pathology." In *The Medical Enlightenment of the Eighteenth Century,* edited by Andrew Cunningham and Roger French, 88–110. New York: Cambridge University Press, 1990.

Gaines, Atwood D., and Paul E. Farmer. "Visible Saints: Social Cynosures and Dysphoria in the Mediterranean Tradition." *Culture, Medicine, and Psychiatry* 10 (1986): 295–330.

García Medina, Pablo. *El método experimental aplicado a la clinica médica.* Bogotá: Imprenta de "La Luz," 1897.

Gayraud, E., and D. Domec. *La capital del Ecuador desde el punto de vista médico-quirúrgico.* Translated by Virgilio Paredes Borja. Quito: Imprenta de la Universidad Central, 1953, orig. pub. 1886.

Gevitz, Norman. "Unorthodox Medical Theories." In *Companion Encyclopedia of the History of Medicine,* edited by W. F. Bynum and Roy Porter, 1:604–12. 2 vols. New York: Routledge, 1993.

Geyer-Kordesch, Johanna. "Georg Ernst Stahl's Radical Pietist Medicine and Its Influence upon the German Enlightenment." In *The Medical Enlightenment of the Eighteenth Century,* edited by Andrew Cunningham and Roger French, 67–87. New York: Cambridge University Press, 1990.

Gibson, William Duke. *The Constitutions of Colombia.* Durham, NC: Duke University Press, 1948.

Glass-Coffin, Bonnie. *The Gift of Life: Female Spirituality and Healing in Northern Peru.* Albuquerque: University of New Mexico Press, 1999.

Golden, Grace. "Juan de Dios and the Hospital of Christian Charity." *Journal of the History of Medicine and Allied Sciences* 33 (1978): 6–34.

González, J. "Medicinal Plants in Colombia." *Journal of Ethnopharmacology* 2:1 (1980): 43–47.

Good, Byron J. *Medicine, Rationality, and Experience: An Anthropological Perspective.* New York: Cambridge University Press, 1994.

Greenfield, Sidney M. "The Return of Dr. Fritz: Spiritist Healing and Patronage Networks in Urban, Industrial Brazil." *Social Science and Medicine* 24:12 (1987): 1095–1108.

Guatemala Indigena (Instituto Indigenista Nacional), 12:1–2 (1977).

Guerra, Francisco. "Medical Education in Iberoamerica." In *The History of Medical Education*, edited by C. D. O'Malley, 419–62. Berkeley: University of California Press, 1970.

———. "The Role of Religion in Spanish American Medicine." In *Medicine and Culture*, edited by F. N. L. Poynter, 179–88. London: Wellcome Institute of the History of Medicine, 1969.

Gutiérrez de Pineda, Virginia. *Medicina tradicional de Colombia: Magía, religión y curanderismo.* 2 vols. Bogotá: Universidad Nacional de Colombia, 1985.

Guzmán Urrea, María del Pilar. "La alopatía y la homeopatía en el siglo XIX: Conflicto entre dos prácticas médicas." *Anuario Colombiano de Historia Social y de la Cultura* 22 (1995): 59–73.

Hamburger, S. "Profile of Curanderos: A Study of Mexican Folk Practitioners." *International Journal of Social Psychiatry* 24:1 (1978): 19–25.

Haro Alvear, Silvio Luis. *Shamanismo en el Reino de Quito.* Quito: Editorial Santo Domingo, 1973.

Harrison, Ira E., and Sheila Cosminsky. *Traditional Medicine: Implications for Ethnomedicine, Ethnopharmacology, Maternal and Child Health, Mental Health, and Public Health—An Annotated Bibliography of Africa, Latin America, and the Caribbean.* New York: Garland, 1976.

Harrison, Ira E., and D. W. Dunlop. *Traditional Healers: Use and Non-Use in Health Care Delivery.* East Lansing, MI: The African Studies Center, 1974–75.

Hassaurek, Friedrich. *Four Years among Spanish Americans.* London: Sampson, Low, Son, and Marston, 1868.

Hays, J. N. *The Burdens of Disease: Epidemics and Human Response in Western History.* New Brunswick, NJ: Rutgers University Press, 1998.

Helquera, J. León. "Chiquinquira." In *Encyclopedia of Latin American History and Culture*, edited by Barbara A. Tenenbaum, 2:143. 5 vols. New York: Charles Scribner's Sons, 1996.

Hernández Colón, Sandra. "The Traditional Use of Medicinal Plants and Herbs in the Province of Pedernales, Santo Domingo." *Arbeits Gemeinschaft Ethnomedizin und H. Buskeverlag* (Hamburg) 4:1–2 (1976–1977): 139–66.

Hernández Sáenz, Luz María. *Learning to Heal: The Medical Profession in Colonial Mexico, 1767–1831*. New York: Peter Lang, 1997.

Hess, David J. *Spirits and Scientists: Ideology, Spiritism, and Brazilian Culture*. University Park: Pennsylvania State University Press, 1991.

Hidalgo Gamarra, Eduardo. "Desenvolvimiento de la medicina en el Ecuador." In *Primer Congreso Médico Ecuatoriano: Actas y trabajos*, 190–95. Guayaquil: Imprenta Nacional, 1916.

Hill, Robert M. "Instances of Maya Witchcraft in 18th-Century America." *Medical Anthropology Quarterly* 1:4 (December 1987): 355–93.

_____. "Instances of Maya Witchcraft in the 18th-Century Totonicapan Area." *Estudios Culturales Maya* 17 (1988): 269–93.

Holden, William Curry. *Teresita*. Illustrated by José Cisneros. Owings Mills, MD: Stemmer House, 1978.

Hollenbach, Margaret. "Culture and Madness: A Colombian Case Study." Ph.D. diss., University of Washington, 1978.

Holton, Isaac F. *New Granada: Twenty Months in the Andes*. New York: Harper and Brothers, 1857.

Ibáñez, Pedro María. *Crónicas de Bogotá*. 4 vols. Bogotá: Biblioteca de Cultura Popular, 1951.

_____. *Memorias para la historia de la medicina en Santafé de Bogotá*. Bogotá: Imprenta Nacional, 1968.

Instituto Geográfico "Agustín Codazzi." *Diccionario geográfico de Colombia*. 2 vols. Bogotá: Banco de la República, 1971.

Janzen, John M. "The Comparative Study of Medical Systems as Changing Social Systems." *Social Science and Medicine* 12:2B (1978): 121–29.

Kempf, Judith. "The Politics of Curing among the Coaiquer Indians." In *Political Anthropology in Ecuador: Perspectives from Indigenous*

Cultures, edited by Jeffrey Ehrenreich, 107–28. Albany, NY: Society for Latin American Anthropology and The Center for the Caribbean and Latin America, SUNY-Albany, 1985.

Kleinman, Arthur. "Concepts and a Model for the Comparison of Medical Systems as Cultural Systems." *Social Science and Medicine* 12 (1978): 85–95.

————. *Patients and Healers in the Context of Culture: An Exploration of the Borderland between Anthropology, Medicine, and Psychiatry.* Berkeley: University of California Press, 1980.

Kroeger, Axel. "South American Indians between Traditional and Modern Health Services in Rural Ecuador." *Bulletin of the Pan American Health Organization* 16:3 (1982): 242–54.

Laguerre, Michel. *Afro-Caribbean Folk Medicine.* South Hadley, MA: Bergin and Garvey, 1987.

Langdon, E. Jean. "Power and Authority in the Siona Political Process: The Rise and Demise of the Shaman." In *Political Anthropology in Ecuador: Perspectives from Indigenous Cultures*, edited by Jeffrey Ehrenreich, 129–56. Albany, NY: Society for Latin American Anthropology and The Center for the Caribbean and Latin America, SUNY-Albany, 1985.

Lanning, John Tate. "The Illicit Practice of Medicine in the Spanish Empire in America." In *Homenaje a Don José María de la Peña y Camara*,143–79. Madrid: Ediciones José Porrua Turanzas, 1969.

————. *The Royal Protomedicato: The Regulation of the Medical Professions in the Spanish Empire.* Edited by John Jay TePaske. Durham, NC: Duke University Press, 1985.

Larco Noboa, Nicolás, Juanita Rebeca Larco Noboa, Santiago F. Larco Noboa, and Patricio Jarrín Molina. *Historia de la medicina ecuatoriana.* Quito: n.p., 1990.

Laviana Cuetos, María Luisa. "Un proceso por brujería en la costa ecuatoriana a fines del siglo XVIII: La Punta de Santa Elena." *Anuario de Estudios Americanos* 46 (1989): 93–129.

Lawrence, C. H. *Medieval Monasticism: Forms of Religious Life in Western Europe in the Middle Ages.* 2nd ed. New York: Longman, 1989.

Lawrence, Ghislaine. "Surgery (Traditional)." In *Companion Encyclopedia of the History of Medicine*, edited by W. F. Bynum and Roy Porter, 2:968–72. 2 vols. New York: Routledge, 1993.

Leacock, Seth, and Ruth Leacock. *Spirits of the Deep: A Study of an Afro-Brazilian Cult.* Garden City, NY: Doubleday Natural History Press, 1972.

Levine, Robert M. *Vale of Tears: Revisiting the Canudos Massacre in Northeastern Brazil, 1893–1897.* Berkeley: University of California Press, 1992.

Lindberg, David C. *The Beginnings of Western Science: The European Scientific Tradition in Philosophical, Religious, and Institutional Context, 600 B.C. to A.D. 1450.* Chicago: University of Chicago Press, 1992.

López Hermosa, Luis. *Bibliografía histórica médica mexicana, 1970–1974.* Mexico City: Sociedad Mexicana de Historia y Filosofía de la Medicina, 1975–1979.

Loux, Françoise. "Folk Medicine." In *Companion Encyclopedia of the History of Medicine,* edited by W. F. Bynum and Roy Porter, 1:665. 2 vols. New York: Routledge, 1993.

Low, Setha M. "Dr. Moreno Cañas: A Symbolic Bridge to the Demedicalization of Healing." *Social Science and Medicine* 16:5 (1982): 527–31.

———. "The Medicalization of Healing Cults in Latin America." *American Ethnologist* 15:1 (February 1988): 136–54.

Loy, Jane Meyer. "Modernization and Educational Reform in Colombia, 1863–1886." Ph.D. diss., University of Wisconsin, 1969.

Luttrell, Anthony. "The Earliest Hospitallers." In *Montjoie: Studies in Crusade History in Honour of Hans Eberhard Mayer,* edited by Benjamin Z. Kedar, Jonathan Riley-Smith, and Rudolf Hiestand. Aldershot, England: VARIORUM, 1997.

Luz Alvarez, M. de la, M. Teresa Araneda, Elisa Fiqueroa, and Soledad Osorio. "Tratamiento de enfermedades en una población rural: ¿Vigencia de elementos hispánicos?" *Social Science and Medicine* 17:8 (1983): 471–74.

Macklin, June. "Belief, Ritual, and Healing: New England Spiritualism and Mexican-American Spiritism Compared." In *Religious Movements in Contemporary America,* edited by Irving I. Zacesty and Mark P. Leon, 383–417. Princeton, NJ: Princeton University Press, 1974.

_____. "Folk Saints, Healers and Spiritist Cults in Northern Mexico." *Revista/Review Interamericana* 3 (1974): 351–67.

_____. "Two Faces of Sainthood: The Pious and the Popular." *Journal of Latin American Lore* 14:1 (1988): 67–91.

Madero Moreira, Mauro. *Historia de la medicina en la provincia del Guayas.* Guayaquil: Imprenta de la Casa de la Cultura, 1955.

_____. *Voces, uso y costumbres del folklore médico ecuatoriano.* Guayaquil: Casa de Cultura, 1967.

Madiedo, Manuel María. *Un eco de Hahnemann en los Andes.* Bogotá: n.p., 1863.

Majno, Guido. *The Healing Hand: Man and Wound in the Ancient World.* Cambridge, MA: Harvard University Press, 1977.

Margolies, Luise. "The Canonization of a Venezuelan Folk Saint: The Case of José Gregorio Hernández." *Journal of Latin American Lore* 14:1 (1988): 93–110.

_____. "José Gregorio Hernández: The Historical Development of a Venezuelan Popular Saint." *Studies in Latin American Popular Culture* 3 (1984): 28–46.

Marina Villatoro, Elba. "Vida y obra de los curanderos de El Petén." *La Tradición Popular* 38 (1981): 1–18.

Marks, Shula. "What Is Colonial about Colonial Medicine? And What Has Happened to Imperialism and Health?" *Journal of the Social History of Medicine* 10:2 (1997): 205–19.

McKee, Lauris. "Ethnomedical Treatment of Children's Diarrheal Illnesses in the Highlands of Ecuador." *Social Science of Medicine* 25:10 (1987): 1147–55.

Menéndez, Eduardo L. *Poder, estratificación y salud: Análisis de las condiciones sociales y económicas de la enfermedad en Yucatán.* Mexico City: Centro de Investigaciones y Estudios Superiores en Antropología Social, 1981.

Millones, Luis. "Shamanismo y política en el Perú colonial: Los curacas de Ayacucho." *Boletín Antropología de América* 15 (July 1987): 93–103.

Miranda Canal, Nestor. "Apuntes para la historia de la medicina en Colombia." *Ciencia, Tecnología y Desarrollo* 8:12 (January–June 1984): 1–265.

Moerman, Daniel E. "Physiology and Symbols: The Anthropological Implications of the Placebo Effect." In *The Anthropology of Medicine: From Culture to Method*, edited by Lola Romanucci-Ross, Daniel E. Moerman, and Laurence R. Tancredi, 129–43. 2nd ed. New York: Bergin and Garvey, 1991.

Moncayo, Pedro. *El Ecuador de 1825 y 1875: Sus hombres, sus instituciones y sus leyes.* 2 vols. Quito: Editorial Casa de la Cultura Ecuatoriana, 1979.

Monteserrat Figueras, Sebastián. *Las actividades médico-castrenses de la inclita orden hospitalaria de San Juan de Dios.* Madrid: Julio Soto, 1950.

Montes Giraldo, José Joaquín. *Medicina popular en Colombia: Vegetales y otras sustancias usadas como remedios.* Bogotá: Instituto Caro y Cuervo, 1981.

Naranjo, Plutarco. "Hallucinogenic Plant Use and Related Indigenous Belief Systems in the Ecuadorian Amazon." *Journal of Ethnopharmacology* (Elsevier Sequoia, Lausanne, Switzerland) 1:2 (April 1979): 121–45.

———. "Medicina indígena y popular de América Latina y medicina contemporanea." *Guatemala Indígena* 13:1–2 (1978): 186–219.

———. "Psychedelic Drugs in Magical Medicine." *Cuadernos Cientificos CEMEF* 4 (1975): 73–92.

Ness, Robert, Gretel H. Pelto, and Pertti J. Pelto. "Alternative Curing Strategies in a Changing Medical Situation." *Medical Anthropology* 3 (Summer 1977): 25–54.

Newberry, Sara Josefina. "Vigencia de las antiguas formas de curar en tres partidos de la provincia de Buenos Aires: Ayacucho, Madariaga y Rauch." In *Informe del Instituto Nacional de Antropología: Formas culturales tradicionales en el área pampeana.* Buenos Aires: Instituto Nacional de Antropología, 1978.

Nutton, Vivian. "Humoralism." In *Companion Encyclopedia of the History of Medicine*, edited by W. F. Bynum and Roy Porter, 1:281–82. 2 vols. New York: Routledge, 1993.

Obregón Torres, Diana. *Sociedades científicas en Colombia: La invención de una tradición, 1859–1936.* Bogotá: Banco de la República, 1992.

———. "Struggling against Leprosy: Physicians, Medicine, and Society in Colombia, 1880–1940." Ph.D. diss., Virginia Polytechnic Institute and State University, 1997.

Orellana, Sandra L. "Aboriginal Medicine in Highland Guatemala." *Medical Anthropology* 1:1 (Winter 1977): 113–56.

———. *Indian Medicine in Highland Guatemala: The Prehispanic and Colonial Periods.* Albuquerque: University of New Mexico Press, 1987.

Pappas, Gregory. "Some Implications for the Study of the Doctor/ Patient Interaction: Power, Structure, and Agency in the Works of Howard Waitzkin and Arthur Kleinman." *Social Science and Medicine* 30:2 (1990): 199–204.

Parédes Borja, Virgilio. *Historia de la medicina en el Ecuador.* 2 vols. Quito: Editorial Casa de la Cultura Ecuatoriana, 1963.

Pareja y Díez Canseco, Alfredo. *Ecuador, la república de 1830 a nuestros días.* 6th ed., corrected and enlarged. Quito: Editorial Universitaria, 1979.

Paz Otero, Gerardo. "Medicina colonial en Popayán." *Boletín Cultural y Bibliográfico* 10:3 (March 1967): 515–29.

Pedersen, Duncan. "Curanderos, divinidades, santos y doctores: Elementos para el análisis de los sistemas médicos." *América Indígena* 49:4 (September–December 1989): 635–63.

Pedersen, Duncan, and Veronica Baruffati. "Healers, Dieties, Saints and Doctors: Elements for the Analysis of Medical Systems." *Social Science and Medicine* 29:4 (1989): 487–96.

Pedersen, Duncan, and Carlos Coloma. "Traditional Medicine in Ecuador: The Structure of Non-Formal Health Systems." *Social Science and Medicine* 17:17 (1983): 1249–56.

Pedersen, Duncan, Carlos Coloma, and Veronica Baruffati. "Health and Traditional Medicine Cultures in Latin America and the Caribbean." *Social Science and Medicine* 21:1 (1985): 5–12.

Pedraza M., Hector. *La enfermeria en Colombia: Reseña histórica sobre su desarrollo.* Bogotá: Editorial Minerva, 1954.

Perdiguero, Enrique. "Protomedicato y curanderismo." *Dynamis* 16 (1996): 91–108.

Perdomo Neira, Miguel. *La iglesia católica en presencia del siglo XIX.* Bogotá: Imprenta de Nicolas Pontón, 1872.

Pérez Arbelaez, E. "Plantas medicinales más usadas en Bogotá." *Suplemento Boletín de Agricultura* 32 (1934): 1–112.

Pergola, Federico. *Brujos y cuasi médicos en los inicios argentinos.* Buenos Aires: EDIMED, 1986.

Pineda Camacho, Roberto. *Historia oral y proceso esclavista en el Caquetá.* Bogotá: Fundación de Investigaciones Arqueológicas Nacionales, 1985.

Pinzón, Martín Alonso. *Historia del conservatismo.* Bogotá: Ediciones Tercer Mundo, 1979.

Planz, Manfred, and Heinrich Keupp. "A Sociological Perspective on Concepts of Disease." *International Social Science Journal* 29:3 (1980): 386–96.

Pollak-Eltz, Angelina. *La medicina popular en Venezuela.* Caracas: Biblioteca de la Academia Nacional de la Historia, 1987.

Porter, Roy. "The Eighteenth Century." In *The Western Medical Tradition: 800 B.C. to A.D. 1800,* edited by Lawrence I. Conrad, Michael Neve, Vivian Nutton, Roy Porter, and Andrew Wear, 371–475. Cambridge: Cambridge University Press, 1995.

———. "Religion and Medicine." In *Companion Encyclopedia of the History of Medicine,* edited by W. F. Bynum and Roy Porter, 2:1452. 2 vols. New York: Routledge, 1993.

Pouchelle, Marie-Christine. *The Body and Surgery in the Middle Ages.* Translated by Rosemary Morris. Cambridge: Polity Press, 1990.

Press, Irwin. "Problems in the Definition and Classification of Medical Systems." *Social Science and Medicine* 1:14B (1980): 45–57.

———. "The Urban Curandero." *American Anthropologist* 73 (1971): 742–56.

Price, Richard. "Kwasimukamba's Gambit." *Brijdragen tot de taal -, Land- en Volkenkunde. Koninklijk Instituut voor Taal-, Land- en Volkenkunde* (Leiden, The Netherlands) 35:1 (1979): 151–69.

Price, Robin. *An Annotated Catalogue of Medical Americana in the Library of the Wellcome Institute for the History of Medicine.* London: Wellcome Institute for the History of Medicine, 1983.

Quevedo V., Emilio. *Historia social de la ciencia en Colombia: Medicina (1)—Institucionalización de la medicina en Colombia, 1492–1860, Antecedentes de un proceso.* 9 vols., 7. Bogotá: Instituto Colombiano para el Desarrollo de la Ciencia y la Tecnología José de Caldas, 1993.

————. "José Celestino Mutis y la educación médica en el Nuevo Reino de Granada." *Ciencia, Tecnología y Desarrollo* 8:1–4 (January–December 1984): 69–114.

Quezada, Noemí. "The Inquisition's Repression of *Curanderos.*" In *Cultural Encounters: The Impact of the Inquisition in Spain and the New World*, edited by Mary Elizabeth Perry and Anne J. Cruz, 37–57. Berkeley: University of California Press, 1991.

Ramírez, Axel. *Bibliografía comentada de la medicina tradicional mexicana, 1900–1978.* Mexico City: IMEPLAM, 1978.

Rappaport, Herbert, and Margaret Rappaport. "The Integration of Scientific and Traditional Healing." *American Psychologist* 36:7 (1981): 774–81.

Risse, Guenter. "Medicine in New Spain." In *Medicine in the New World: New Spain, New France, and New England*, edited by Ronald L. Numbers, 12–166. Knoxville: University of Tennessee Press, 1987.

————. "Medicine in the Age of Enlightenment." In *History of Medicine in Society: Historical Essays*, edited by A. Wear, 149–95. Cambridge: Cambridge University Press, 1992.

Rivas, Medardo. "Perdomo." *Obras de Medardo Rivas: Parte primera.* Bogotá: n.p., 1883.

Robinson, Scott S. "Banisteria and Lophophora: Some Intriguing Implications." In *Estudios sobre etnobotánica y antropología médica II*, edited by Carlos Viesca Treviño, 169–76. Mexico City: IMEPLAM, 1977.

Rodríguez Freyle, Juan. *El carnero*, edited by Dario Achury Valenzuela. Caracas: Biblioteca Ayacucho, 1979.

Romano V., Octavio Ignacio. "Charismatic Medicine, Folk Healing, and Folk-Sainthood." *American Anthropologist* 67 (1965): 1151–73.

Rosenberg, Charles. "Introduction: Framing Disease—Illness, Society, and History." In *Framing Disease: Studies in Cultural History*, edited by Charles E. Rosenberg and Janet Golden, xiii–xxvi. New Brunswick, NJ: Rutgers University Press, 1992.

Rosselli, Humberto. "Relación de médicos y notables empíricos." *Médicos* 3 (1979): 55–72.

Rota, Domingo. *Casos felices y auténticos de medicina.* Tunja: Vicente de Bañus, 1830.

Rubel, Arthur J., Carl W. O'Neill, and Rolando Collado. "The Folk Illness Called *Susto*." In *The Culture-Bound Syndromes: Folk Illnesses of Psychiatric and Anthropological Interest*, edited by Ronald C. Simons and Charles C. Hughes, 333–67. Dordrecht, The Netherlands: B. Reidel, 1985.

Rumbaut, Ruben D. *John of God: His Place in the History of Psychiatry and Medicine*. Miami, FL: Ediciones Universal, 1978.

Ryn, Zdzislaw. *Los Andes y la medicina*. La Paz: Instituto Boliviano de Cultura, 1981.

Safford, Frank. *The Ideal of the Practical: Colombia's Struggle to Form a Technical Elite*. Austin: University of Texas Press, 1976.

Salomon, Frank. "The Fury of Andrés Arévalo: Disease Bundles of a Colonial Andean Shaman." In *Political Anthropology of Ecuador*, edited by Jeffrey Ehrenreich, 83–105. Albany, NY: Society for Latin American Anthropology and the Center for the Caribbean and Latin America, SUNY-Albany, 1985.

Samaniego, Juan José. *Cronología médica ecuatoriana*. Quito: Editorial Casa de la Cultura Ecuatoriana, 1957.

Sandoval, Mercedes C. "*Santería* as a Mental Health System: A Historical Overview." *Social Science and Medicine* 13B:2 (April 1979): 137–51.

Santos Granero, Fernando. "Power, Ideology and the Ritual of Production in Lowland South America." *Man* 21:4 (December 1986): 657–79.

Sarkís, Alia, and Víctor Manuel Campos. *Curanderismo tradicional del costarricense*. San José: Editorial Costa Rica, 1978.

Shaman. *Medicina y economía: Un estudio de la evolución histórica de la relación entre medicina y estructura socioeconómica en el Ecuador*. Quito: n.p., 1979.

Silverblatt, Irene. "The Evolution of Witchcraft and the Meaning of Healing in Colonial Andean Society." *Culture, Medicine, and Psychiatry* 7 (1983): 413–27.

Silverio, Manco. *La doctrina de la madre María: Cómo la difundía para curar las enfermedades del cuerpo y del alma (consideraciones científicas)*. Buenos Aires: Editorial Caymi, 1974.

Simoni, Joseph J. "Can We Learn from Medicine Hucksters?" *Journal of Communication* 25:3 (1975): 174–81.

Siraisi, Nancy G. *Medieval and Early Renaissance Medicine: An Introduction to Knowledge and Practice.* Chicago: University of Chicago Press, 1990.

Sodiro, Luis. *Una excursión botánica.* Quito: Imprenta Nacional, 1881.

———. *Contribuciones al conocimiento de la flora ecuatoriana.* Quito: Tipografía de la Escuela de Artes y Oficios, 1900.

Soriano Lleras, Andrés. *Crónica del hospital de San Juan de Dios desde su fundación hasta su administración por la Junta de Beneficencia de Cundinamarca, 1654–1869.* Bogotá: Junta General de Beneficencia de Cundinamarca, 1964.

———. *La medicina en el Nuevo Reino de Granada, durante la conquista y la colonia.* Bogotá: Editorial Kelly, 1972.

Sowell, David. " 'La teoría i la realidad': The Democratic Society of Artisans of Bogotá, 1847–1854." *Hispanic American Historical Review* 67:4 (November 1987): 611–30.

Talbott, John A. *A Biographical History of Medicine: Excerpts and Essays on the Men and Their Work.* New York: Grune and Stratton, 1970.

Taussig, Michael. "Folk Healing and the Structure of Conquest in Southwest Colombia." *Journal of Latin American Lore* 6:2 (Winter 1980): 271–78.

———. *Shamanism, Colonialism, and the Wild Man: A Study in Terror and Healing.* Chicago: University of Chicago Press, 1987.

Tedlock, Barbara. "An Interpretive Solution to the Problem of Humoral Medicine in Latin America." *Social Science and Medicine* 24:12 (1987): 1069–84.

Temkin, Owsei. *Hippocrates in a World of Pagans and Christians.* Baltimore, MD: Johns Hopkins University Press, 1991.

TePaske, John Jay. "José Celestino Mutis," in *Encyclopedia of Latin American History and Culture*, edited by Barbara A. Tenenbaum, 5:150–51. 5 vols. New York: Simon Shuster Macmillan, 1996.

Trotter, Robert T., II. "Curanderismo: An Emic Theoretical Perspective of Mexican-American Folk Medicine." *Medical Anthropology* 4:4 (1980): 428–88.

Trotter, Robert T., II, and Juan Antonio Chavira. *Curanderismo: Mexican American Folk Healing.* Athens: University of Georgia Press, 1981.

Troya, José María. *Vocabulario de medicina doméstica*. Quito: Tipografía de la Escuela de Artes y Oficios, 1898.

Turner, Bryan S. *Medical Power and Social Knowledge*. Beverly Hills, CA: Sage, 1987.

Ulrich, Laurel Thatcher. *A Midwife's Tale: The Life of Martha Ballard, Based on Her Diary, 1785–1812*. New York: Vintage Books, 1990.

Universidad Nacional de Colombia, Centro de Bibliografía y Documentación. *Tésis existentes en la Biblioteca de la Facultad de Medicina*, edited by Lucía Belmonte Román. Bogotá: Ciudad Universitaria, 1964.

Uribe Angel, Manuel. *La medicina en Antioquia*. Bogotá: Editorial Minera, S.A., 1936.

Uricoechea, Fernando. "La institucionalización de la práctica científica en Colombia." *Ciencia, Tecnología y Desarrollo* 8:1–4 (1984): 39–55.

Van der Geest, Sjaak. "Christ as Pharmacist: Medical Symbols in German Devotion." *Social Science and Medicine* 39:5 (1994): 727–32.

Vanderwood, Paul J. *The Power of God against the Guns of Government: Religious Upheaval in Mexico at the Turn of the Nineteenth Century*. Stanford, CA: Stanford University Press, 1998.

Vargas Lesmes, Julián, and Guillermo Vera Pardo. "Formas asistenciales y de beneficencia en Santafé: Hospitales, expósitos y hospicios." In *La sociedad Santa Fé Colonial*, edited by Julián Vargas Lesmes, 255–97. Bogotá: CINEP, 1990.

Vasco de Escudero, Grecia. *Directorio ecuatoriano de archivos*. Quito: Instituto Panamericano de Geografía e Historia, 1979.

Viesca Treviño, Carlos. "La medicina tradicional mexicana." In *Memorias del símposio medicina tradicional, curanderismo y cultura popular en Colombia de hoy: Curanderismo, parte 1°*, by the Instituto Colombiano de Antropología, 13–23. Bogotá: Seríe Memoria de Eventos Científicos-ICFES, 1990.

Vila de Pineda, Patricia. "Algunos aspectos del estudio de la medicina tradicional en Colombia." In *Memorias del símposio medicina tradicional, curanderismo y cultura popular en Colombia de hoy: Curanderismo, parte 1°*, by the Instituto Colombiano de Antropología, 25–34. Bogotá: Seríe Memoria de Eventos Científicos-ICFES, 1990.

Weibe, Robert. *The Search for Order, 1877–1920*. New York: Hill and Wang, 1967.

Weinstein, Donald, and Rudolph M. Bell. *Saints and Society: The Two Worlds of Western Civilization, 1000–1700*. Chicago: University of Chicago Press, 1982.

Woods, Clyde M. "Alternative Curing Strategies in a Changing Medical Situation." *Medical Anthropology* 1:3 (Summer 1977): 25–54.

Wright, Peter, and Andrew Treacher. *The Problem of Medical Knowledge: Examining the Social Construction of Medicine*. Edinburgh: Edinburgh University Press, 1982.

Yépez Villalba, Eduardo. *150 años de la Facultad de Medicina: 1827–26 de octubre 1977*. Quito: Editorial Universitaria, 1979.

Young, Allan. "The Dimensions of Medical Rationality: A Problematic for the Psychosocial Study of Medicine." In *Toward a New Definition of Health*, edited by Pal Ahmed and George Coelho, 67–85. New York: Plenum Press, 1979.

Zuñiga Cisneros, M. "España, la medicina religiosa y los hospitales." *Archivo iberoamericano de historia de la medicina y antropología médica* 8 (1956): 377–86.

INDEX

Latin American Silhouettes
Studies in History and Culture

William H. Beezley and
Judith Ewell
Editors

Volumes Published

(1998). Cloth ISBN 0-8420-2716-5 Paper ISBN 0-8420-2717-3

Brian Loveman, *For* la Patria: *Politics and the Armed Forces in Latin America* (1999). Cloth ISBN 0-8420-2772-6 Paper ISBN 0-8420-2773-4

Guy P. C. Thomson, with David G. LaFrance, *Patriotism, Politics, and Popular Liberalism in Nineteenth-Century Mexico: Juan Francisco Lucas and the Puebla Sierra* (1999). ISBN 0-8420-2683-5

Robert Woodmansee Herr, in collaboration with Richard Herr, *An American Family in the Mexican Revolution* (1999). ISBN 0-8420-2724-6

Juan Pedro Viqueira Albán, trans. Sonya Lipsett-Rivera and Sergio Rivera Ayala, *Propriety and Permissiveness in Bourbon Mexico* (1999). Cloth ISBN 0-8420-2466-2 Paper ISBN 0-8420-2467-0

Stephen R. Niblo, *Mexico in the 1940s: Modernity, Politics, and Corruption* (1999). Cloth ISBN 0-8420-2794-7 Paper (2001) ISBN 0-8420-2795-5

David E. Lorey, *The U.S.-Mexican Border in the Twentieth Century* (1999). Cloth ISBN 0-8420-2755-6 Paper ISBN 0-8420-2756-4

Joanne Hershfield and David R. Maciel, eds., *Mexico's Cinema: A Century of Films and Filmmakers* (2000). Cloth ISBN 0-8420-2681-9 Paper ISBN 0-8420-2682-7

Peter V. N. Henderson, *In the Absence of Don Porfirio: Francisco León de la Barra and the Mexican Revolution* (2000). ISBN 0-8420-2774-2

Mark T. Gilderhus, *The Second Century: U.S.-Latin American Relations since 1889* (2000). Cloth ISBN 0-8420-2413-1 Paper ISBN 0-8420-2414-X

Catherine Moses, *Real Life in Castro's Cuba* (2000). Cloth ISBN 0-8420-2836-6 Paper ISBN 0-8420-2837-4

K. Lynn Stoner, ed./comp., with Luis Hipólito Serrano Pérez, *Cuban and Cuban-American Women: An Annotated Bibliography* (2000). ISBN 0-8420-2643-6

Thomas D. Schoonover, *The French in Central America: Culture and Commerce, 1820–1930* (2000). ISBN 0-8420-2792-0

Enrique C. Ochoa, *Feeding Mexico: The Political Uses of Food since 1910* (2000). ISBN 0-8420-2812-9

Thomas W. Walker and Ariel C. Armony, eds., *Repression, Resistance, and Democratic Transition in Central America* (2000). Cloth ISBN 0-8420-2766-1 Paper ISBN 0-8420-2768-8

William H. Beezley and David E. Lorey, eds., *¡Viva México! ¡Viva la Independencia! Celebrations of September 16* (2001). Cloth ISBN 0-8420-2914-1 Paper ISBN 0-8420-2915-X

Jeffrey M. Pilcher, *Cantinflas and the Chaos of Mexican Modernity* (2001). Cloth ISBN 0-8420-2769-6 Paper ISBN 0-8420-2771-8

Victor M. Uribe-Uran, ed., *State and Society in Spanish America during the Age of Revolution* (2001). Cloth ISBN 0-8420-2873-0 Paper ISBN 0-8420-2874-9

Andrew Grant Wood, *Revolution in the Street: Women, Workers, and Urban Protest in Veracruz, 1870–1927* (2001). ISBN 0-8420-2879-X

Charles Bergquist, Ricardo Peñaranda, and Gonzalo Sánchez G., eds., *Violence in Colombia, 1990–2000: Waging War and Negotiating Peace* (2001). Cloth ISBN 0-8420-2869-2 Paper ISBN 0-8420-2870-6

William Schell, Jr., *Integral Outsiders: The American Colony in Mexico City, 1876–1911* (2001). ISBN 0-8420-2838-2

John Lynch, *Argentine Caudillo: Juan Manuel de Rosas* (2001). Cloth ISBN 0-8420-2897-8 Paper ISBN 0-8420-2898-6

Samuel Basch, M.D., ed. and trans. Fred D. Ullman, *Recollections of Mexico: The Last Ten Months of Maximilian's Empire* (2001). ISBN 0-8420-2962-1

David Sowell, *The Tale of Healer Miguel Perdomo Neira: Medicine, Ideologies, and Power in the Nineteenth-Century Andes* (2001). Cloth ISBN 0-8420-2826-9 Paper ISBN 0-8420-2827-7

June E. Hahner, ed., *A Parisian in Brazil: The Travel Account of a Frenchwoman in Nineteenth-Century Rio de Janeiro* (2001). Cloth ISBN 0-8420-2854-4 Paper ISBN 0-8420-2855-2

Richard A. Warren, *Vagrants and Citizens: Politics and the Masses in Mexico City from Colony to Republic* (2001). ISBN 0-8420-2964-8

Roderick J. Barman, *Princess Isabel of Brazil: Gender and Power in the Nineteenth Century* (2002). Cloth ISBN 0-8420-2845-5 Paper ISBN 0-8420-2846-3